HELPING TEENS
with Stress, Anxiety, and Depression

"Working in youth ministry for more than two decades, I've seen firsthand the effects that growing stress and anxiety are having on our children, teens, and young adults. The reality and severity of this problem cannot be exposed or confronted enough. I'm so thankful for this new book by Roy Petitfils. He tackles a pervasive dilemma head on by pulling from his own life experience, relevant statistics, his substantial ministry experience, and the timeless wisdom of the Bible and the Church. Petitfils not only outlines the challenges we face while helping young souls but also provides a practical road map for anyone to help and guide teens who are struggling. The result is a valuable tool for every parent, pastor, and youth leader charged with leading young souls to freedom and, ultimately, to heaven. This is a great gift to our Church."

Mark Hart
Executive Vice President, Life Teen International

"Many people know Roy Petitfils as a speaker and counselor with expertise in pastoral and clinical arenas. As his friend, I see a passion and drive behind the scenes that most won't. No one works harder in terms of research, staying current with adolescent culture, and doing his own self-work. This book is a welcome and needed resource that springs from his passion, personal mission, and genuine desire to equip adults with knowledge and practical tools to step in when our caring desire is not enough. This is a wonderful guide to help us be more confident and competent as we accompany teens."

Mike Patin
Catholic speaker, facilitator, and consultant

"It is hard to navigate the difference between teenage woes and deeper issues that need attention. In this practical and information-packed book, Roy Petitfils gives adults an in-depth look at how to recognize when teens are in trouble and then step in to help with effective tools from best practices in mental health care and the rich spiritual traditions of the Catholic Church."

Elizabeth Madeo
Director of Faith Formation, Annunciation Parish

HELPING TEENS

with Stress, Anxiety, and Depression

A FIELD GUIDE FOR CATHOLIC PARENTS, PASTORS, AND YOUTH LEADERS

ROY PETITFILS

AVE MARIA PRESS AVE Notre Dame, Indiana

Founded in 1865, Ave Maria Press is a ministry of the United States Province of Holy Cross.

www.avemariapress.com

Paperback: ISBN-13 978-1-59471-889-2

E-book: ISBN-13 978-1-59471-890-8

Cover and text design by Brianna Dombo.

Printed and bound in Canada.

Library of Congress Cataloging-in-Publication Data is available.

CONTENTS

PREFACE

In the movie *Pirates of the Caribbean: At World's End*, Captain Barbossa says, "For certain, you have to be lost to find a place that can't be found."

Accompanying today's young people can feel like being lost. Adults often feel unsure of what to say, how to help, or what to do when they are concerned about a teen. As one adult recently told me, "I don't want to say the wrong thing, risking the kid thinking that I just don't get it, and yet I'm worried that saying nothing may tell 'em I don't care."

The prospect of venturing deeper into the emotional lives of young people to try to direct them can feel disorienting. In addition to the normal emotional rollercoaster of adolescence, the new stressors teens face today can make them feel they're in an emotional house of mirrors with worries, stresses, and fears dancing and multiplying.

The prospect of helping teens sort through the emotional ups, downs, and turnarounds they experience can be daunting, even for seasoned parents, educators, ministers, and other caring adults.

This leaves us in an interesting place: anxious and fearful adults tasked with helping anxious and fearful young people. At first glance, this might seem an impossible mess. Yet the more aware we are of our own fears and concerns, the more we will be able to relate to young people. The substance of our worries may be different, but we will meet them from a place of common experience, which ultimately strengthens our potential to help.

"BE NOT AFRAID"

In both the Old and New Testaments, our God reminds us that we have nothing to fear. In fact, "be not be afraid" is one of the most repeated phrases in the Bible. Like me, perhaps there have been times when you've heard that phrase and thought, *Yeah, right! That's easy for God to say.*

The truth is that God designed us to experience both fear and calm, each in the right amount at the right time. The trick is knowing how much is enough, how much is too much, and how much is too little. Many youth and adults alike are experiencing too much stress and too little peace. But how do we change? How do we help young people cope with stress and anxiety and discover more of God's peace? Answering that question is the purpose of this book.

PIECES OF MY JOURNEY

One of the reasons I have such a heart for teens today is that as a teen I struggled. I *really* struggled.

Like 34 percent of young people in America today, I was raised by my mom, a single parent. And like 15 percent of today's youth, I was born in poverty. My mom's faith was important to her, but like so many parents I've worked with over the years, she felt inadequate about passing it down to me. So for my mom, getting a good Catholic education was the key to breaking the cycle of poverty and me becoming a good Catholic man. Growing up I watched her work four jobs in order to make that happen: sixteen-hour days, six or seven days a week, often leaving me home alone to fend for myself after school. I didn't realize it then, but I was hurting. The sadness and loneliness were maddening, and at an early age, I turned to food to cope with my emotional pain. Food was my companion when no one was there.

One day in my second year of high school, my mom picked me up from school, which never happened because she normally worked till long after dark and got home after I was in bed. We drove to a local grocery store and went straight to the meat counter where we were greeted by a large, red-haired, red-bearded butcher wearing a bloodstained white coat. Waving us back with a bloody meat cleaver, he said, "Y'all come on back." I asked my mom, "What are we doing here?" She said, "Your doctor called today to get an accurate weight on you." "So why didn't we go to his office?" I asked. "Because," my mom said, "you haven't been able to weigh on the doctor's scale since you were in eighth grade. It only goes up to 350 pounds."

So at sixteen years old I was trying to wrap my mind around the fact that I weighed more than 350 pounds. The butcher points to a massive scale used to weight large portions of meat that haven't yet been portioned for retail sale.

"Get on up there, Roy," he said. "Let's get a weight on ya." I emptied my pockets and took off my shoes (don't we all?) and stepped up to watch a long red needle zip around and land on 454. I heard my mom gasp and then watched as the shame, embarrassment, and powerlessness trickled down her cheeks.

Through a choked-up voice my mom said, "We've gotta do something about this, baby."

"I know, Mom," I said.

But we didn't.

Mom kept working and I kept eating. I gained even more weight. Like so many children under eighteen, I grew up in poverty.[1] As a poor, morbidly obese child, I was bullied for those reasons and more. I dreaded school and was absent as often as my mom would allow to avoid being bullied. The defenses I used to protect myself only brought more negative attention my way. I hated myself as a teenager and contemplated suicide many times.

There were adults who tried to help and saw part of my struggle. But in general, I felt invisible to my peers and my teachers. I was the largest human being in my hometown, and I felt as if I was wearing Harry Potter's invisibility cloak. I graduated near the bottom of my class, weighing more than five hundred pounds and donning a 7X shirt with a size 64-inch waist. I hated myself. At seventeen years old I often thought, *Why would people like me? I'm just poor, fat, and stupid.*

I basically flunked out of college and got a job in industrial construction. After about a year, I went back to college with the help of coworkers. My first day back on campus a group of guys I'd known in high school approached me saying, "Hey, Roy, you need to come to the Catholic student center." To that I replied, "I haven't been to church since tenth grade, and I don't plan on starting now." They smiled and said, "But there are *free donuts.*" I said, "Well . . . I guess I should at least check it out." God often uses carbs to draw us closer to himself!

I stopped going to church in tenth grade because my mom, while wanting me to go, wasn't around enough to make me. I wasn't aware of it at the time, but I harbored a deep resentment toward God. Like many youth, I didn't think God was as capricious and vengeful as much as apathetic to my situation and unable—or even worse, unwilling—to help me.

When I walked into the Catholic student center, I discovered heaven: boxes upon boxes of hot, fresh donuts. To the shock and horror of many regulars, I strutted up, grabbed my dozen, and plopped down into a small sofa that fit me like a chair, shattering one of its legs. A few students came to talk with me. I instantly made my mission clear: I was only there to eat one dozen donuts; hold the religion please.

They pressed on, asking me about myself and seeming genuinely interested in me. Many of our initial conversations revolved around me, which made me feel weird and awkward, as it can for so many young people desperately wanting positive attention. Because I couldn't get much positive attention, when I did it seemed to arbitrarily come in short spurts. I had long settled for negative attention, because it seemed to come more easily. But these people seemed genuinely interested in me. Unlike in high school, they really saw *me*, and I began thinking, *Maybe there's more to me than I can see.*

I continued going to the Catholic student center, mainly for food and friendship, still keeping the religion at bay. No one forced it on me or even pushed it. I was pretty interested in it, though, because the people I met at the center were genuinely happy. I tried to convince them (and myself) that I was happy, but the truth was I was miserable. I was anxious and severely depressed for most of my teen years, and while things were now going more in my favor, I was still depressed. I still hated myself.

Fifteen years later, the priest at the student center, who is now a dear friend, told me, "When I saw you on the couch that day, I'd never seen someone who hated themselves as much as you did. And I fell in love with you" (in a healthy, safe, environment-approved way). He and so many others at that place loved me into loving myself. I had poor social skills, and while I was taught good southern manners, I'd fallen off the wagon of politeness and was smelly, unkempt, and foul-mouthed. I embarrassed people. I said and did things I shouldn't have. I was not easy to love. But they loved me anyway.

I began paying closer attention to how these people interacted, how they lived. They were *truly* happy—not the kind of happy of the much-too-perky morning person you want to punch in the trachea. They would have good days and bad days, but there was something special about what made their good days good and what got them through the bad days. It was immediately clear to me that there was something about reaching out to, connecting with, and helping other people while accepting help from others that contributed to their peace and genuine joy.

I started going back to church with them. I began asking questions about my faith, and they patiently answered. We had spirited debates, but they didn't leave me, which was something I always feared. I was always scared to be truly honest with people because I was afraid they would stop liking me and leave.

Going back to the sacraments, especially Eucharist and Reconciliation, were game changers for me. I noticed that the more consistently I showed up to church, the more consistent was my healing and, dare I say it, my growing sense of happiness. I also began meeting with the priest. He helped me get a nutrition coach, a gym membership, and counseling—at first with him and then with a licensed therapist.

I began losing weight, and over the next two years I continued meeting with the priest, who gave me much-needed counsel and spiritual direction, and developed lifelong friendships and deep bonds with several people from that Catholic student center. These people are now my best friends, and one of them is my wife. In that two-year period, I lost nearly three hundred pounds without bariatric surgery.

Although I wasn't completely aware of what I was learning at the time, the young adult me discovered the keystones of healthy living for me: proper rest, healthy nutrition, exercise, journaling, silence, prayer, spiritual direction, counseling, and participation in the sacramental and communal life of the Church. I discovered that these practices, many of which may sound very secular, were all elements of my Catholic faith. That faith became the cornerstone that held my life together.

Many, upon hearing my story, say, "You should have been on the *Biggest Loser*" (a dramatic show featuring contestants who lose significant weight in a short period of time). In fact, I was the "biggest winner" because my dramatic physical transformation and subsequent ability over the next twenty years to maintain it is symptomatic of a much deeper, more significant spiritual transformation.

I cannot help but be compassionate toward young people today, having experienced what I did in my youth. I saw the difference caring adults made in my life, how those adults, both physically and spiritually, saved my life. That has inspired me over the last twenty years to attempt to give back to young people the gifts that were given to me.

IN THE TRENCHES

Over the last two decades, I've worked with young people in a variety of settings, including in schools, parishes, and private practice as a psychotherapist. I've watched young people in the throes of worry, anxiety, and depression make decisions to improve their situations. Many of them discover that at some point in their struggle they turned away from the one person who could help them most: God. I've watch countless youth reopen their hearts to God and allow God's grace, working through their own decisions and disciplines and with assistance from other people, cope with stress and discover more peace, hope, and happiness.

In addition to working with young people themselves, I've sat with their parents, trying to understand how their kid who had "everything" wanted to end his life; how a kid who had "nothing to worry about" was so riddled with anxiety it affected her body's ability to function normally; how an extroverted college freshman couldn't find a way to leave his dorm room for weeks because he was afraid to fail; how an adolescent girl's perfectionism and subsequent anxiety nearly cost her the success she'd worked her whole life to achieve; and how a child who seemed so interested in the faith is now a professed atheist or agnostic.

In addition to these young people and their families, I've also had countless opportunities to consult with their teachers, administrators, professors, and ministers who feel powerless facing the ever-increasing complexity and magnitude of emotional issues today's youth experience. I've heard their frustration and desperate cries for better tools and new applications of older tools so they can help youth and their families find peace and joy amid chronic and often severe stress, anxiety, and depression.

I've watched young people apply the principles I'll share with you in this book and discover emotional and spiritual freedom. I've watched adults grow in confidence as they feel more helpful to young people after incorporating a new tool or technique.

You won't find formulas in this book, as human relationships tend to defy any formulaic approach. You will find principles that you can apply regardless of your situation or the circumstances of your teens. You will find language that can help you open up dialogue with a closed-off young person.

HOW TO READ THIS BOOK

As an avid reader, I always appreciate the author giving me permission to jump around the book, so I'm giving you that gift as well. Look over the table of contents to find subjects that are relevant to your particular context or situation. If your teen is depressed, you may want to dive right in to chapter 5, "Recognizing Anxiety and Depression." If your teen is particularly stressed, you may want to start in chapter 4, "Understanding Stress," or chapter 6, "Avoiding the Undue Pressures of Success."

The chapters are laid out in an order that facilitates a sequential approach as well. Some of the information in the later chapters will build upon principles and techniques laid out in the beginning. Most importantly, highlight the language, tips, and tools that resonate with you. Get what you can as quickly as you can from this resource. Don't be afraid to earmark or bookmark pages or passages to revisit.

DIGITAL RESOURCES

In each chapter you'll find a few instances where I've offered you the opportunity to discover additional content. These resources may be videos, PDF files, or a more detailed description of the topic being considered. For the majority who will be reading a paperback in their hands, the exact links will be offered in the chapter notes.

KEY POINTS AND ASK YOURSELF

Each chapter will conclude with what I believe are the key points. These aren't the only key points, but they are at least a few. Look them over and don't be afraid to add to them. In addition, take a few minutes to reflect on the questions at the end of each chapter. You might consider writing your responses as a way of deepening your learning.

SCRIPTURE AND PRAYER

The scripture passages are provided to offer the following:

1. *Hope.* Sometimes knowing that what we're experiencing with a young person is talked about in scripture gives us hope. It can help knowing that our unique experiences also have a common element shared by others who have gone before us.
2. *Encouragement.* God's Word can help us to press on when we feel discouraged and are tempted to give up.

3. *Opportunity for prayer.* Take a moment or two to pray with the passage and listen to what God might be saying uniquely to you and your situation.

TAKE ACTION

Not everything you read will be helpful or applicable to your situation or context. You'll no doubt find at least a few tips, tools, and insights that will. Act on those. Put them into practice right away. Share them with a friend or colleague.

The worst thing that could happen as a result of you reading this book is to find it interesting and insightful but do nothing with it. Use what you'll learn here to help you reach out, reconnect with, and accompany the young people in your life through the tough times they're likely facing.

WITH A GRATEFUL HEART

The word "book" is a simple way of describing a massive, complex project that involves multiple teams of people. This section exists in order to thank, in a published and printed document, those individuals who make up the team responsible for getting a book from just a "good idea" to a physical and final published piece.

I have to start by thanking my beautiful wife, Mindi, who, still today, after seventeen years of marriage, is my best friend. Thank you, my love, for your unwavering support from the very beginning of this project and for your encouragement throughout all of my doubts and thoughts about quitting or postponing, including giving me seven days away in a beachfront condo in Gulf Shores, Alabama, to finish the manuscript. When I asked for your blessing to take the time and invest the money in this vacation, you immediately, without hesitation, said, "Absolutely." You and I both knew that the household chores and managing our family's active schedule would fall squarely on your shoulders, only months into a new position for you at your workplace. Thank you for being the parent who manages the lives of our boys while I'm away counseling, speaking, or writing to help everyone else's kids.

I'm grateful to my sons, Max and Ben, who, like their mom, make countless sacrifices when I get on planes without them to go speak to other kids. I know at times they wish they had their daddy all to themselves. Your support meant more to me than you two probably knew at the time. And I couldn't do the ministry I do without your support and love. Both of you are by far the most significant and important young people in my life. I pray you never forget that!

My friend, mentor, and colleague Dan Jurek, LMFT, has for more than twenty years now been my youth minister, boss, friend, brother, father figure, and now associate at Pax Renewal Center, a Catholic counseling center of which I'm privileged to be a part. You have and continue to influence me in ways that each day make me a better man, husband, father, and, most importantly, son of God. Without your enthusiastic support for this project, I'd have most likely not taken it on. Special thanks for encouraging me to get away in May 2018 for seven days, which is really hard to do for a teen counselor in May. Thanks for your support and encouragement.

My brother, friend, and mentor Mike Patin continues to teach me about ministry, work ethic, professionalism, and countless practical suggestions for helping young people. I'm ever grateful for your suggestions over the years that help me craft the message and teach it in ways that are most helpful to those who serve young people. Thank you for the many times you've heard me speak on this subject and for your brilliant, grace-inspired suggestion to frame pastoral care within the context of the parable of the Good Samaritan, which is highlighted in chapter 10. I have the gift of making simple things complicated. You have a well-honed gift of making things that are complex and inaccessible (like this sentence) accessible to people who desperately need this information and need to use it.

Thanks go also to my editor, Eileen Ponder. I was having strong doubts about whether to continue with this project, unsure of my ability to invest the time in the writing, rewriting, revising, and then rewriting and revising some more. When I saw what you did with my initial table of contents and introduction, how accessibly and beautifully you shaped the content while keeping my own voice, I was convinced this project could be an exceptional work and a valuable resource for parents, educators, and ministers. I am truly grateful, honored, and privileged to have worked with you.

The incredible staff at Ave Maria Press immediately saw the potential in this work and committed to it quickly and without reservation. Thank you for everything you do to make this book beautiful, exceptional, useful, and widely available and accessible to those who need it.

Lacie, my assistant at Pax Renewal Center, crosses the t's and dots the i's in my counseling practice and at Today's Teenager. I'm grateful that you make it easier and easier for me to do what I do best, which is connect, create, and communicate.

Tori helped with the massive amounts of research needed to write this book and labored to read my handwriting while making editorial corrections. Thanks, Tori!

My friend Chris Meaux, a good writer himself, produces the Today's Teenager podcast, which has featured much of the content in this book. Thanks for your help with the chapter reflection questions, scriptures, and prayers to make the book even more useful.

Thanks also go to Kevin Dore, Dr. Danielle Dore, Christine Dore, Roy and Amy Provost, and Rob and Denise Utter for generously supporting the ministry of Today's Teenager. This book, the podcasts, the blogs, and so many talks were made possible through your generosity.

To my clients and the many young people and their families over the years who have taught me and helped me way more than I can imagine I've ever helped you, thank you for allowing me into your lives, your hearts, and your minds. Thank you for teaching me about your experience so that others realize they are not alone.

May 3, 2018
Gulf Shores, Alabama

PART I

OUR FIELD OF
ENGAGEMENT

1. HOW BIG IS THE PROBLEM?

"Roy, do you really think the mental health problems with young people today are as big as some are making it out to be? I mean, is it that things are that much worse, or do we just know more than we once did?" This question from a friend is one I'm asked often. It suggests that the psycho-spiritual state of today's youth may be no better or worse than it was fifty years ago, but now, due to advances in technology and access to unprecedented amounts of research and information, we may be identifying a problem and its magnitude that has long been present yet unidentified.

It's hard to answer such questions with empirical certitude. I suspect the truth, as in most things, is somewhere between the two extremes. Spiritual, emotional, and psychological distress in young people has always been an element of adolescence, yet societal taboos, lack of research funding (due to lack of awareness of the significance of the problem), and limited access to information made it hard to comprehend and respond to teens in earlier generations. On the other hand, the particular ways in which these problems are presenting themselves has changed and is currently changing at a pace many of us who work with young people are finding hard to keep up with. And there is solid research to suggest we are indeed facing unprecedented challenges in helping teens respond to mental health issues.

WHAT DO WE KNOW?

Anxiety

The National Institute of Mental Health reports that 31.9 percent of adolescents have had an anxiety disorder, making it the most commonly diagnosed mental health disorder in America today for teens. Most adults I encounter as I speak and consult across the world tell me they are seeing not only this trend but also teens experiencing more and more anxiety, stress, and worry over the last five to ten years. This seems to be most acute in developed countries such as the United States.[1] In chapter 5 we'll discuss the various reasons for this sharp increase.

Depression

In 2016 the National Institute of Mental Health reported that approximately 3.1 million young people aged twelve to seventeen experienced a major depressive episode (they were clinically depressed); this represents nearly 13 percent of the US population in this age group. Of those young people, 19 percent are female compared to 9 percent males.

Suicide

According to the Centers for Disease Control and Prevention, the suicide rate for young people aged ten to seventeen has increased 70 percent between 2006 and 2016.[2] Nearly 9 percent of teens attempt suicide each year (of teens who report having attempted suicide).[3] As of this writing, in the United States, suicide ranks as the second-leading cause of death for young people aged twelve to nineteen.[4]

Self-Injury

On average, one in five teens "self-injures," meaning they intentionally harm themselves by way of cutting, carving, burning, extreme hair pulling, punching themselves, scratching, or hitting something with a part of their body intended to cause harm.[5] Most young people aren't born wanting to hurt themselves. Self-injurious behavior is a symptom of a deeper problem, most often stress, anxiety, or depression.

Eating Disorders

Disordered eating, such as anorexia nervosa and bulimia, affect roughly one in ten teens. Young people with an eating disorder often experience other problems as well, such as anxiety, depression, and self-injurious behavior. This is not a problem that only affects females.

LGBTQ+

In case you aren't familiar with the acronym, LGBTQ+ stands for lesbian, gay, bisexual, transgender, queer or questioning, and (+) other nontraditional, male or female gender orientations or sexual orientations.

Regardless of how you feel or what you believe about these issues and the people who identify with them, these young people are at a significantly higher risk for anxiety, depression, self-injury, eating disorders, and suicide. The suicide rate for LGBTQ+ youth is ten times higher than for the rest of the population.

Bullying

Approximately 21 percent of young people aged twelve to eighteen experience bullying,[6] with 160,000 teens each day missing school because of bullying.[7] This could easily be a chicken-or-egg-type question, but suffice it to say this is a meaningful statistic indicating a problem among today's young people. Bullying is often the cause of absenteeism.

Disaffiliation from Religion

In the United States, an increasing number of families are divorcing from religion and in some cases God altogether. In surveys of religious affiliation, the largest group today is "unaffiliated." This ever-growing group of Americans who choose not to affiliate with any particular religion or denomination aren't necessarily atheists or agnostics. They just don't want to participate in organized religion. Knowing that religious practice and affiliation can be for many a source of hope, inspiration, and calm, it is not a leap to conclude that the lack of what used to be a readily available coping mechanism—that is, faith and religious affiliation/practice—is leading to higher levels of stress, anxiety, and depression in our country today. This is also easy to observe in other developed nations.

It would be easy to look at the numbers and assume there's a relationship between religious disaffiliation and rising mental health concerns among young people. I've found that to be the case. I'm not suggesting that youth who are religious, go to church, and pray don't have problems, even serious problems. What I am suggesting is that I've seen young people begin struggling, get confused as to why God isn't "showing up" or "answering their prayers," and then, often unconsciously, begin drifting away from personal prayer, other devotions, and even communal participation. We'll discuss in detail in chapter 7 how we can help young people find renewed strength in religion even when they previously searched but couldn't find the help they were looking for.

Family Issues

The nature and shape of the American family has changed drastically over the last few decades. The traditional family as once understood— a father and mother married once with one or more children whom they physically bore, where Dad worked and Mom stayed home to raise children and manage the household—exists today in fewer than 7 percent of homes. I'm not suggesting that the traditional family was without flaw, nor do I suggest that young people from traditional families were and are immune to pressures and challenges. But these changing dynamics are affecting young people in ways we do know about, such as increased stress, anxiety, and depression, and also in ways we are still discovering.

Divorce

The divorce rate continues to hover around 50 percent. Many young people say that their parents' fighting or divorce doesn't bother them. Some who have good coping skills and a healthy diversified support system (multiple assets) survive divorce relatively unscathed. For others without a good support system, it can be a nightmare. The challenges of divorce for young people are complicated by the fact that many of today's teens resist acknowledging the problem for fear of appearing too cliché. Take my client Sam who was severely depressed at fifteen years old. He initially stated, as do many teens, "My parents' divorce didn't affect me. We don't need to talk about that. I'm not this angsty teen who hates my parents because they decided to get a divorce. It's fine. I'm okay and they're better off without each other." For Sam and roughly half of the youth in America, their parents' divorce doesn't make them special because so many others are going through the same thing. Teens often dismiss the distress that divorce causes them simply because it is so common. Over time, Sam would eventually share how scared he felt when his parents would fight and how alone he felt during and after the divorce.

Adoptive Families

Each year more than 150,000 young people are adopted in the United States. In 2015 there were nearly 1.5 million youth in adoptive families.[8] Like any other setting that has potential challenges, adoptive families do too. There are young people who begin and end their lives filled with gratitude for the amazing life being adopted gave to them and never once question their origins and identity. They seem not to experience any severe emotional challenges. Yet for many adopted youth, it can be tough.

Jaley (age 14) said, "I love my mom and dad," referring to her adoptive parents. "They have given me a life I'd have never had in Russia. But I want to know not where I come from but *who* I come from. It doesn't happen often, but when I see a friend who resembles their mom or dad, I get sad 'cause I know I'll never get that." Jaley, like all adopted kids, is at a heightened risk for adverse mental health problems. She continued, "It helps that I can talk about this with my parents who listen without getting defensive when I'm sad or upset. I know how big a deal that is, Roy. My friend is adopted too, and his parents get all butthurt when he asks about his birth parents, telling him how grateful he should be. He's like, 'I am grateful! *And* I want to know who my birth mom is.' I guess I'm lucky."

Foster Families

There are more than 450,000 young people in foster care in the United States.[9] Many of these young people know who their birth parents are. Some young people wish they could be with them, and many others are grateful to be out of the situation they were in. For Alex (age 9), the stress of being in the foster system caused severe anxiety. He'd have multiple panic attacks every day. Talking helped. One day he told me, "I just want to stay somewhere. I just never know when they'll send me back (to his birth parents), or I dunno if these people want to keep me. I try to be real good so they want me and my little sister."

Blended Families

Sarah (age 10) whose parents divorced and remarried, lives in a blended family, as do 67 percent of youth from divorced homes. These are families that have been combined from two previously existing relationships. Sarah says, "I've learned that family is what you define it to be. No one gets to tell you what family means to you. I've got four parents and consider myself lucky." For her it is a great experience. For Josh (age 15) it's not. "How is it I'm the only one who didn't get a vote. Mom and Dad voted and their boyfriend and girlfriend voted, but I didn't get a vote. Now I'm supposed to 'get on board' and pretend to love and like these two new people who aren't my mom and dad. And I'm supposed to treat them like they are? No thanks."

Kids will each experience blended families differently. What's important for us adults who care for and support them is to be aware that kids in blended families represent a large percentage of youth, and it can be a significant stressor that puts them at risk for other problems.

Single Parents

About 34 percent of young people live in single-parent homes in the United States. As in many of the nontraditional family settings young people are in, this is often a better situation than what these young people previously knew. That being said, the pressures of one parent trying to do the job of two take a toll on both parent and child. I watched my single mom work more and stress more because there wasn't another adult at home to share the multitude of responsibilities that come with raising children. Today, I'm married with two kids, and I don't know how she did it. I have the deepest respect for single parents, many of whom didn't make the choice to be a single parent or who felt compelled to make that choice so they could put themselves and their children in better, safer places.

Grandparents Raising Grandchildren

In 2016 the Pew Foundation reported that 2.9 million grandchildren were being raised by their grandparents.[10] Hilda's daughter was in and out of rehab so often that Hilda felt obligated to give her grandchildren some sense of stability. So she took them into her home and assumed joint custody of them along with her daughter. "Raising one set of kids when you're younger is tough enough, much less doing it again during your golden years, years I once dreamed I'd have more time for. Don't get me wrong, Roy. I *love* these kids like they were my own—I guess 'cause they are. But I wanted to love them as a grandparent, not a mom. I know it's tough for them too. I just don't have the energy to keep up with middle school kids, and I'm afraid when they get to high school, me going to events for them and with them will be embarrassing for them."

Now, I know many grandparents who can outrun and outwork me any day! But setting and maintaining boundaries with a child or a teenager is tough. Yet most young people want to be raised by healthy birth or adopted parents and are affected when that's not possible for a variety of reasons including, but not limited to, a parent's death, physical illness, serious mental illness, or an otherwise lack of capacity to parent effectively.

Same-Sex Marriages and Relationships

Nearly 200,000 youth live in homes with a same-sex couple, and between 2 and 3.7 million young people in the United States have at least one parent who identifies as lesbian, gay, bisexual, transgender, or questioning.[11] As one young man told me, "I think it's cool that my dad and his partner are together and that they are my parents. But there are times when it's a little weird and embarrassing."

~~~~~~~~~~~~~~~

The notion of "family" is being radically redefined for this current Generation Z as well as the millennials before them. Many believe that family transcends blood relationships and extends beyond the physical boundaries of their home and extended blood relations. To be sure, there are positive benefits to this emerging reality. For example, when John's parents were arguing, he was able to reach out to his friends, what some call the "second family," for crucial support and encouragement. John says, "I love my mom and dad. But I can't count on them. I never know when they'll blow up or what they'll blow up about. I know I can count on my friends."

There are also obvious drawbacks for young people counting on friends as their primary means of support. Sure, kids will naturally pull away from parents and rely on their friends. But when a young person, especially an adolescent, who by nature will have vacillating moods and a shifting identity, depends too heavily on friends, problems often arise. Friendships often shift quickly and unexpectedly in adolescence, leaving vulnerable teens open to disappointment and sometimes crushing feelings of failure and isolation. As Katie says, "I really thought I could count on them. I made sure they always could count on me. But when I needed them the most, they weren't there." As adults, it's somewhat easy to understand the limited emotional availability an adolescent can offer. But for young people, it's as if the rug got pulled out from under them. When this happens, teens often feel their whole world is falling apart.

IS THERE REASON TO HAVE HOPE?

Glancing at these statistics can be disheartening and truly scary. Really pondering them can be especially distressing for us who care about, live with, or work with young people. But we are not alone in our desire to help, nor are we without hope.

We all know the highlight of the parable of the prodigal son: boy wants independence, asks Dad for money, which he then squanders. When the reality of his plight hits him, the son returns home to his father's forgiving embrace amid the backdrop of a jealous older brother. That was what I read for decades. But there's one line in the parable that I always managed to miss. "While he was still a long way off, his father caught sight of him, and . . . *ran* to his son" (Lk 15:20, italics added).

I always envisioned the father working on his favorite hobby when his ragged son tapped him on the shoulder from behind and they embraced. But the scripture implies that the father was waiting and looking for him, perhaps even anticipating his arrival. He was watching and, when he saw his son, ran to him.

Our God is a God who wears running shoes. Long before, during, and long after we're fatigued, disheartened, discouraged, sad, hurt, and burnt out, our God reminds us that "our kids" were his first! This parable reminds me that if our omniscient God refuses to give up hope and refuses to be discouraged, maybe I should as well.

These statistics are real. The problems *are real*, and in many ways we're currently scrambling for ways to make it better. This is not cause to lose hope and give in to discouragement. We acknowledge the reality, and we do what we can with whatever resources we have, whatever gifts we have to cooperate with the grace of God in us, the same grace that is also in the young people whom we parent, teach, supervise, minister among, and serve.

Just in case you're still debating whether or not to enter the fray, don't decide until you read the next chapter, "Should I Step In?"

2. SHOULD I STEP IN?

One afternoon, during my second year teaching and directing the campus ministry program at a Catholic high school, I was sitting alone in my classroom when a mentor, Dan, walked into the room. As God would have it, he and I are both counselors today in the practice Dan founded, Pax Renewal Center.

It was painfully obvious that day that I was struggling—maybe because I was crying—and he said, "What's wrong, brother?"

"I don't know what I'm doing," I sobbed. "The kids hate me and I can't teach them anything. They're not signing up for the programs I started, and I dunno, I just feel like a complete failure. I don't know if I'm cut out for working with teens. And I look at Dr. Bollich and Mike Keefe (two veteran teachers) and I mean they *really* know what they're doing. They help these kids. The kids like them and they seem to be able to get through to them. I'll never get there, man."

Dan smiled a smile I've seen many times since. It was the smile that now, as a dad, I know to mean, *I've been there too. And this, as bad as it might seem, will pass.* "Roy, those guys have been doing this for decades. This school already has a Dr. Bollich and a Mike Keefe; it doesn't need another one of either of them. What it needs is a Roy."

As simple as those words might seem, they instantly gave me hope and a boost of self-confidence. Then he said, "Come see me tomorrow and let's talk it through in more detail and see if we can tweak a few things that will make your life easier."

We talked countless times after that. I learned a lot about myself and about how to effectively reach young people. I learned mostly through making countless mistakes, some of which still embarrass me. Like pulling a kid out into the hall and yelling at him because he drank (though didn't get drunk) at a party and had signed a no-drinking contract to be on the retreat team I directed. I didn't just embarrass that young man. I shamed him.

You too will make or have already made mistakes that will tempt you to quit or give up. But try to keep in mind that God does not call the qualified; he qualifies the called. There have been many "Dans" in my life who affirmed me, encouraged me, and gave me valuable tools, tips, and tricks to be more effective in accompanying young people on their journeys.

The *Catechism of the Catholic Church* states, "The desire for God is written in the human heart" (*CCC*, 27). I take comfort in these words. Based on the way I once ministered to young people, you wouldn't have known that. I acted as if it were my job to put God in them.

It helps us sometimes to refer to young people, whether or not they're children or youth whom we minister among, as "our" young people. We do that because we are protective of them, because we care for them. That's okay, as long as we remember that even more deeply than they are ours, they ultimately, like us, belong to God. And as such, he has created them with a homing beacon for himself.

Remember: by accompaniment I mean stepping into kids' hearts and lives, accompanying them by walking alongside them, pointing out pitfalls, and offering suggestions, guidance, and challenge to them to navigate what can be, at times, difficult paths.

Our job isn't to put Jesus in their hearts; it's to help them realize he's already there and help remove the clutter, the debris, and other interference that blocks the sound of God's still small voice within them.

FAITH IS A MUSCLE
THAT NEEDS FLEXING

I'm often asked, "Roy, why are you so darn passionate about adults getting into these messy areas with kids? I mean why can't we just leave that to the psychologists and counselors? That's their job."

This is a legitimate question. We'll get into this in greater depth in chapter 9, "Finding Help for the Helper." I'm not hoping to make professional ministers and volunteers into psychotherapists and social workers (unless that's what you want, and if so you should seek out the formal education and training you need for that). I am convinced that we who are people of faith move into these messy areas because

- Jesus modeled this for us;
- he asked this of us;
- there's a very real need;
- many of the young people in our care would never get formal psychological therapy without our help; and
- most importantly, our involvement in the real messy parts of people's lives says something to them not just about themselves as loveable but also about God's passionate love for them.

Our witness as ministers—filled with compassion, armed with our skills, understanding our roles, and maintaining healthy boundaries—allows God's presence to be experienced in a special way during a difficult time in a young person's life. Sometimes they recognize the encounter while in the messiest of the mess, but more often they see God in our accompaniment when they reflect backward on those hard times.

In many ways we're asking young people to make a leap of faith. It's risky to give one's life to Jesus. It's not safe and neat. Yet after being in ministry for a while, a temptation can sneak into our hearts and minds to mitigate or get rid of all risk, shy away from the unknown, and avoid messy at all costs. To be fair, there are real fiscal responsibilities. We must be good stewards of the resources available to us. But these resources are to be at the service of the Gospel. When our overriding need for security interferes with our ability to live the fullness of Gospel, we must ask ourselves if what we're doing as parents, ministers, social workers, or teachers is worth advanced risk management.

BY STEPPING IN, WHAT AM I WITNESSING TO YOUTH?

Young people know they're not easy to work with, so when they see us giving our time to be with them, they sense there is a deeper reason behind what we're doing. They know they are a mess at times. And so, while they may not consciously acknowledge the witness you provide them, they are usually, at least on an unconscious level, recognizing the sacrifice of your time and asking themselves, "Why would these adults do this? Why would they give of their free time to be with me?"

These questions will often dwell in their hearts for years. The answers may come gradually over time. But our presence among them forces them to hold the questions and ponder them. These inner questions pull them forward with an unknown curiosity into who we are, why we are, and ultimately, who God is. Can our work and witness really be for them?

OUR FAITH IS RELATIONAL

Catholic Christianity is not a head game or a solitary affair. It is relational by its nature. The mystery of the Incarnation makes it this way. Jesus didn't come into the world as might a Greek god; an isolated, narcissistic God; or demigod who was perfectly fine by himself. He came into a family, a region, a religion, and a faith community. He shared his life with others, and they shared with him. In him we see the relational nature of our faith.

When we enter into relationships with young people, we are, even if it doesn't feel like it, in a very real way witnessing to a reality deep in the heart of our faith: God comes to us in and through relationships. We believe that God's very nature is relationship—that God exists as three distinct persons bound together in perfect communion as the Blessed Trinity. And we say that God *is* love. What is love but the best sort of relationship? When we enter into real relationship with our kids, with the young people in our care as parents or other leaders, we participate in a very real way in the life of our triune God.

This is heady stuff I know. I often fall into the trap of seeing my spirituality as a private affair between me and God. In these moments, I act as if my attempts at individual sanctity or growth are most important. There is little evidence in the history of Christianity that this is true. In fact, the exact opposite is true. Most of the great saints in history were men and women whose lives and spirituality reflected deep relationships with others, often they would credit these others for leading them closer to the heart of Christ. It is in and with one another that we encounter and come to know God.

"GO MAKE A MESS"

Not long after he was elected, Pope Francis told the young people at World Youth Day, "Go back home and make a mess." He was encouraging the young people to shake things up in their parishes, to be more assertive about their involvement in parish life. He encouraged them to point out the blind spots, the unseen or unmet needs in their local communities. Essentially, he encouraged them to go back home and make it hard for their pastors and the parish staff to keep doing business as usual.

Francis knows that much of the institutional Church does not like messy. We have diocesan, regional, and parish structures and personnel to make ministry and pastoral life neat and clean. There is much good in this. Boundaries, order, and guidelines give us a sense of security, stability, and predictability.

But that can go too far. This is what our Holy Father is challenging us to see. Our need for order, neatness, clear lines, and control, all good and natural human and institutional needs, have in many areas of Church life taken precedence over other important needs and as such have stifled the Holy Spirit. "The Spirit moves where it will . . ." And sometimes, the Spirit is messy.

I hate messy. Whether it's just my natural personality that loves control or it's part of my OCD, I like it when things are neat and tidy. I hate worrying about loose ends.

In my second year of doing campus ministry, we'd taken a large group of our students to Mexico for a service learning experience. I tried to keep the numbers for the trip down to a "controllable" size, but the interest far outweighed my need for control. Instead of taking one fifty-five-passenger bus, we took two with a small group of parents flying in to meet us. We were almost 120 people total—in a foreign country.

On the way down there, a parent could see I was stressing. I could tell he was as chill as an ice cube. He said, "What's wrong, Roy?"

"Nothing," I said, lying through my teeth.

"Bahahaha! You can't fool me; I know nervous when I see it."

"What do you mean?" I asked.

"Well, I can see you're breathing really hard and you're not relaxed like you normally are. What are you stressing about?"

"How much time you got?" I jokingly asked.

"Well, from the looks of it, about ten more hours," he said.

"All these kids are my responsibility. What if something goes wrong?"

"Yeah. It probably will."

"Huh?"

"Well, chances are, something probably will go 'wrong'; I mean, they're teenagers."

"What do you mean?"

"Well, it's part of being a teen, doing stupid things, and yes, doing things wrong or not fully thought out. So yeah, statistically, and since I'm a numbers guy, by the numbers, something will probably go wrong."

"Yeah . . . I know."

"And what's so bad about that?"

"I'll get in trouble. I should have prevented whatever goes wrong."

He leaned in and said, "Roy, no offense, brother, but you are not God. You aren't that powerful. And besides, anyone who expects real ministry in the lives of teens to be problem free . . . well let's just say, they're off their rocker a tad."

I laughed, digesting his point, which did make me feel better. He went on: "Teens are messy, man. And from what I gather in my limited experience, ministry is messy. I mean, it just seems to me from readin' the Bible that whenever God gets involved in something, he makes a mess out of it."

"I know and that's what scares me."

"Initially!"

"Huh?"

"Initially. It's messy in the beginning because there's a whole lot of change. But then things calm down and from what I gather, things are better than before. Different, maybe scarier, less certain, but better. Now you know the Bible better than me, but isn't that right?"

"I guess you're right."

"Thanks!" he said. "My wife never says that—good to hear sometimes!"

I laughed, thinking the same thing.

That was a powerful lesson: Real Teens + God = Messy. But the mess, instead of signaling that something is wrong, often (though not always) is a sign that something good is happening.

It's much easier to sit at home or drown into an app or game on our phones than to open our eyes and realize that our teens today, as we saw in the last chapter, are really hurting and need our help. Yes, it's messy. Yes, it's scary. But what's the alternative? Do nothing? Pretend it's not happening? Assume that God will send others who are better suited for it? Each of these responses happens every day in our Church and teens are no better for it.

Honestly, I hate the messy part of being involved in the real lives of teens. I hate having to consult, pray, journal, think about it, have difficult conversations, call their parents, cry with them, laugh with them, challenge them, have expectations that go unmet, be disappointed by them, and be angered by them, but that's what it takes. And teens, on some level, understand that's what we're pushing through and dealing with. As one teen told me, "You guys are either crazy, stupid, or heroes; I'm not sure which yet."

STRENGTH OF COMPASSION

It is clear looking at Jesus' ministry that he was filled with compassion for people. In my field of psychotherapy, empathy is a popular concept. In graduate school we're taught how to empathize, or to put ourselves in the shoes of others, to think about how we might feel or act or think if we were in the same situation as that other person. Empathy is an amazing gift and skill that can be learned.

Yet there are times in ministry when, despite our training and gifts, we are unable to empathize with others to the degree we'd like. There are times when, due to lack of energy or personal experience, we just can't seem to understand what another person is going through. In times like those, we're better served by the virtue of compassion.

Compassion and empathy are often used interchangeably. Technically, "empathy" means to feel with and "compassion" means to suffer with. I suggest that compassion is a virtue because we don't get the emotional payoff that we do with empathy. It's easier to help when we have empathy for someone or a particular situation. In our minds we think, *I've been there and I know if it were me I'd want . . .* There's a motivating energy with empathy.

Compassion, on the other hand, is a movement of not only the heart but also the will. It's a test of the will because you may not feel like doing it and you may not have empathy for the person or the situation. This is the type of love Mother Teresa talked about when she said, "We must love until it hurts."

Essentially, compassion means I am making a choice to move into a situation to be with another, to "suffer" with another, even when I am not able to fix the situation. Personally, I love to fix. I'm in a "fixing" profession. Of course, we don't call it that, and most of us abhor the word "fix," especially when our clients ask us to fix them. But I'd be lying if I didn't admit that I like it when what I do makes a difference in a teen's life. I like fixing. Perhaps you do too.

Working with ministers, educators, and parents for many years now, I've learned that many of us are fixers. And as a parent, there aren't too many of us who, at some point or another, don't want to "fix" our kids. This can be both good and bad. It's good to fix the boo-boo on the four-year-old knee, but doing homework for your tenth grader to make sure they don't bomb a class is going too far.

For fixers, compassion can be quite difficult because we don't get the good feeling that we get when we feel we're making a difference. Often, we'll feel nothing but bad, sharing the pain of the one we seek to accompany. This has been a long, painstaking lesson; I'm still learning. As a counselor, there are often teens who are in situations I cannot make better. I can't fix them, and I can't tell the teens how to fix them. The only thing I can do is to be with the teens while they're experiencing the situation and help them keep their head above water until they're old enough to move out of the situation and begin making choices for themselves. That has at times been a long road, often years. It doesn't feel good. And to be honest, I don't have any letters from those teens thanking me for hanging with them, telling me how awesome I was to stay in it with them and how my presence helped them hang on every time they were tempted to lose hope.

What I have heard is that others in the lives of teens who do stick by them make a difference. I hear about *you* every day. All the time, I hear about the parents who patiently put up with the emotional rollercoasters; the ministers who ask about situations they know aren't getting better but want to give the youths a chance to talk about it and let those kids know they're being prayed for and thought about; and the teachers who took a few minutes to ask how a kid was doing, without being intrusive. I hear about you heroes—all the time.

Clearly, the problem is massive. There are times when I look at the numbers and the reality of our current situation with young people and feel discouraged. I'm reminded of a friend who once told me, when I was experiencing a moment of self-doubt about all the hours I was spending away from home and family without seeing "results," which happens so often in ministry, "Roy, if not you, who? I mean how many people do you see lining up who actually like teens and have it on their heart to serve them? Do what you need to do, but don't fool yourself, it's not as if there's a line of more skilled, effective ministers waiting to take your place."

BUT AM I QUALIFIED?

Remember, "God doesn't call the qualified; he qualifies the called." You might be thinking, *Who am I to attempt to meet these serious needs that teens today have?* You might feel insufficient to the task. Too often God puts a desire on our hearts and we rationalize not following that desire because of a lack of skill, resources, education, or training. Those are all important. But without a desire on your heart to accompany our young Church, all of those tools are merely just that—tools. On their own these qualifications can do nothing without a servant's heart that is willing to put them to the right use.

KEY POINTS

- Raising or working with young people and teens is far from easy. It is a messy undertaking because teens are messy by nature.
- To help teens means forming a relationship and entering into the messes of their lives.
- The essence of God is made manifest in the relationship of Father, Son, and Holy Spirit. Jesus modeled relational, incarnational ministry for us and then asked us to do the same for each other.
- There is a real need for compassionate and caring people to help young people with the struggles discussed in the previous chapter.
- Adults taking time to help teens who recognize they're not easy to work with shows teens they are worth time, effort, and, most of all, love.
- Without those willing to build relationships with teens and their parents, many would not get the mental health treatment and care they desperately need.

ASK YOURSELF

1. Which people, both in and out of my family, showed that they genuinely cared about my well-being when I was a teenager? Write their names in a journal or notepad. Think about these

people for a few minutes and the things you most clearly remember about them.

2. In what ways did these adults prove that they had an authentic love and concern for me? List a few of those examples for further reflection.

3. If you are a parent, think about your child's life and consider, Who has touched my daughter's life? My son's? Again, write down their names.

4. Think about the person or people you named in question three and ask yourself, How have I acknowledged their care for my child? How am I demonstrating my gratitude for their decision to get involved with the "messy" lives of young people?

5. If you don't have a young person or teen in your personal life, consider, What are some ways I can become involved in building relationships with teens in my community or in my family?

FOR INSPIRATION AND PRAYER

Do nothing out of selfishness or out of vainglory; rather, humbly regard others as more important than yourselves, each looking out not for his own interests, but [also] everyone for those of others.

Have among yourselves the same attitude that is also yours in Christ Jesus,

Who, though he was in the form of God,
did not regard equality with God something
to be grasped.
Rather, he emptied himself, taking the form
of a slave,
coming in human likeness;
and found human in appearance.
—Philippians 2:3–7

Then the king will say to those on his right, "Come, you who are blessed by my Father. Inherit the kingdom prepared for you from the foundation of the world. For I was hungry and you gave me food, I was thirsty and you gave me drink, a stranger and you welcomed me, naked and you clothed me, ill and you cared for me, in prison and you visited me." Then the righteous will answer him and say, "Lord, when did we see you hungry and feed you, or thirsty and give you drink? When did we see you a stranger and welcome you, or naked and clothe you? When did we see you ill or in prison, and visit you?" And the king will say to them in reply, "Amen, I say to you, whatever you did for one of these least brothers of mine, you did for me."

—Matthew 25:34–40

So, during supper, fully aware that the Father had put everything into his power and that he had come from God and was returning to God, he rose from supper and took off his outer garments. He took a towel and tied it around his waist. Then he poured water into a basin and began to wash the disciples' feet and dry them with the towel around his waist.

—John 13:2b–5

3. HOW CAN I HELP?

There are many of us in the field of youth work. But unless you're already in it we don't have *you*. The Church and our young people need you, because no one else occupies your particular place in the world or has your insight, your smile, your love, and your unique way of caring or your knowledge. God has provided those gifts and intends for you to share them.

I love the fact that you're reading this chapter. It means that on some level, you *want* to help. Or perhaps, like me, you feel that accompanying young people has brought you to a place where you find yourself needing assistance! That's normal and happens to us all at some point. And the truth is, if we are open to it, we can learn from both the adults who help and guide us and from the young people in our care.

I hope you'll find things you need in the pages to come: affirmation, encouragement, and, most of all, practical tools that, more than any pep talk, will help you effectively understand, reach, and ultimately influence young people with the love of God and the saving message of the Gospel.

In the first paragraph of this book, I quoted Captain Barbossa, who said, "For certain, you have to be lost to find a place that can't be found." I always tell adults who feel lost when it comes to understanding young people that feeling lost doesn't necessarily mean they're doing something wrong; it often indicates they're out ahead of the pack, in the dense woods where a trail has not been cleared yet. When you're out there in the lead, you're bound to occasionally question yourself, wondering if you're really headed in the right direction.

So the first task is to educate ourselves about who teens are. How do they mature in all areas of their life? What are their unique pressures? How do family systems work in shaping and developing young people? How is God's grace working in all that mess to make things new through his son, Jesus? Simple, right?

As we progress through the second part of this book, not only will we be tackling difficult issues such as anxiety and depression in greater detail, but also we will be exploring how young people grow and develop physically, psychologically, and spiritually. We will probe how they are affected by contemporary social and cultural challenges as we seek to accompany them in their growth toward happy, holy, healthy, and successful adulthood.

My approach to helping adults help young people has always been threefold: understand, reach, and influence. In the next few chapters we'll focus on understanding young people today and on the skills you need to reach this often apathetic, aloof, and resistant generation of youth. And finally, we will explore how your ability to influence them with the message of the Gospel is directly related to your courage and willingness to step in.

TO UNDERSTAND—GET EDUCATED

If you've ever said yes to something without fully understanding what you were getting into and later regretted it, you'll understand why this section is so important. Young people and the challenges they face have changed and are changing rapidly. If we wish to get through to them, it is important that we make it a priority to expand and update our existing knowledge of teens, their culture, and their unique challenges.

Understanding Stress

As we've established, young people are under unprecedented amounts of stress. This seems to infiltrate every aspect of their lives: peer relationships, schooling, family life, career aspirations, and economic stability or the lack thereof, not to mention the social and political churnings of recent years. In chapter 6 we'll examine what stress is and how it fits into God's design for our lives so that we can better understand the unhealthy, toxic, and chronic stress that so many young people today are experiencing. We'll discuss how when young people experience too much unhealthy stress it can affect their hearts and minds, which ultimately affects their ability to experience calm, peace, and real happiness.

Recognizing Anxiety and Depression

We'll also look at the warning signs for both anxiety and depression, two serious mental health problems that a significant number of young people face today. You'll learn how stress can cause both of them and the unique "fraternal twins" nature of anxiety and depression. This is important because either one left unattended can lead to the other and perhaps even more serious problems.

Avoiding the Undue Pressures of Success

"I just want my kid to be successful, Roy." This is a lament I hear too often from parents that are worried about their kids who may or may not be in counseling. They're worried that they're not doing the right things or that they did the wrong things and messed up their kids. Educators face similar, but different, pressures to give young people the tools they will need to be successful in a rapidly changing world. Ministers and other caring adults are trying their best to help young people embrace God in their lives while also balancing success-driven schedules. In this chapter, we'll examine the word "success" and the meaning it has for many young people and their families. We'll take a challenging look at how today's common definition of success holds up in comparison to the light of the Gospel of Jesus Christ.

TO REACH—GET COMFORTABLE

Have you ever given advice to a teen only to see eyes rolled back, or hear "Yeah, but . . ." (followed by some reason your advice won't work)? This is because you didn't fully reach or connect with that teen. In our enthusiasm to help teens as much and as quickly as possible, we often rush in with advice before making the connection. You've no doubt heard the cliché "meet them where they're at." This part of the book will give you the practical tools to help you do that and help you to know if and when you've effectively reached the teen.

Using the Roadmap of Catholic Faith

In chapter 7 we'll look at the tools that are readily available within the rich traditions of our Catholic faith, tools such as prayer, ritual, community, sacraments, and discipline, to name but a few. We'll see how Catholicism, considered antiquated by many today, is perhaps the best option and should be first in the line of defense in curtailing serious problems for young people when they do arise. We'll explore how faith helps people address and cope with the various problems and stressors that will inevitably come to the surface. We'll also talk about how we can impart these helpful tools of faith in such a way that young people will integrate them into the fabric of their lives.

Learning the Art of Listening

You might imagine that this was my favorite chapter to write, since I am by profession a counselor. And you are correct. I may even need to write a whole book on this one day! In chapter 8, arguably the most important, we'll discover how something each of us do every day, listening—something seemingly so passive that it often feels we're doing nothing—can truly transform the life of a young person.

TO INFLUENCE-GET COURAGEOUS

Understanding and reaching teens on their own are not enough. Our goal is to share the Good News of Jesus Christ with them, to help them. Our efforts at understanding and reaching pave the way for us to help them, to influence them.

In the final chapters we'll shift our attention to taking action and look at the courage needed to move intentionally into the areas of young people's lives that are messy, disordered, and scary. We'll discuss how the virtues of empathy and compassion are similar yet distinct and how both are necessary in being a courageous caring adult.

Finding Help for the Helper

It's only fitting that at the end of a whole book on pastorally caring for others, we also look at what it means to take care of *yourself.* The old axiom remains true today: You can't give what you haven't first received. To truly understand, reach, and influence young people, we need to be actively taking care of ourselves. This doesn't mean we need to be perfect, spotless, and without our own struggles. In fact, it seems at times that God works most powerfully through us when we feel we are at our lowest.

By reading this book, you're taking a massive step. So many young people don't get the support they need and end up falling away from Church and God because the adults in their lives lacked some basic understanding of adolescent psycho-spiritual development.

KEY POINTS

- If you're not already working with young people today, it's not too late to begin, and they need you. You offer insight, experience, and gifts unique to you.
- Key to helping young people today is understanding the unprecedented, toxic, and chronic stress that is one of the main causes of the anxiety they face.
- Adults willing to work with young people must also recognize the warning signs of both anxiety and depression and how stress creates these forces.
- It is critical to understand how the various pressures to succeed, whether from others or the young people themselves, create tremendous stress for teens.

- Helping young people define success in healthy ways must be informed by the Gospel.
- Our Catholic faith as embodied in fellowship, sacraments, and ritual can be a tool not only in helping struggling young people but also for the well-being of adults seeking to work with teens.
- Simply listening well to young people, with compassion and without judgment, can make a huge difference in their lives.

ASK YOURSELF

1. How did I define success as a young person? Is that definition still valid, or has it changed as I have with time, experience, and growth?
2. Who influenced my definition of success when I was a teen?
3. Was the idea of success suggested by the adults in my life positive or negative?
4. How did these adults primarily encourage me to pursue success?
5. How might I offer my experience and insight as a "former teen" to the young people of my community and church parish?
6. What would be required for me to become involved in one of the opportunities I listed in the previous question?

FOR INSPIRATION AND PRAYER

Know this, my dear brothers: everyone should be quick to hear, slow to speak, slow to wrath, for the wrath of a man does not accomplish the righteousness of God.
—James 1:19–20

For lack of guidance a people falls;
security lies in many counselors.
—Proverbs 11:14

Standing by the cross of Jesus were his mother and his mother's sister, Mary the wife of Clopas, and Mary of

Magdala. When Jesus saw his mother and the disciple there whom he loved, he said to his mother, "Woman, behold, your son." Then he said to the disciple, "Behold, your mother." And from that hour the disciple took her into his home.

—John 19:25–27

PART II

THE TOOLS OF
ENGAGEMENT

4. UNDERSTANDING STRESS

John was a self-described "stress head." "I get it from my dad," he'd often say. "I don't know why but we both get stressed out a lot."

On the huge white board in my office I drew a long line, indicating a continuum. On one side was "no stress," and on the other side it said "too much stress." I asked John to take the marker and mark two spots: one spot for where he was at the time and one for where he wants to be. He marked spots at both ends of the continuum, indicating he felt he was too stressed but wanted no stress.

"I see you are *here* now," I said, pointing to the *too much stress* side, "but," I said, as I pointed to the *no stress* side, "why do you think you need to be all the way over there?"

"I dunno," he said (the most repeated phrase I hear from young people).

"Let's pretend you're all the way on the other end."

"Okay."

"If there were something about being all the way over on the *no stress* side that kept you from getting there, what would it be?" With most people, boys especially, admitting fear is a sign of weakness and feels vulnerable. When you ask it hypothetically, as I did when I said "let's pretend," you've got a better chance of getting the teen to acknowledge it.

"I don't think it's scary," he said. I expect that response about half the time.

"Oh, I didn't think it was for you." I drew a stick figure to signify we're talking about someone else. I pointed to the figure and asked, "What if Jack *had* to be scared of something over here?" I asked, pointing to the *no stress* end. "What *would* it be?"

"I guess being all the way over there would mean he's not trying."

"And what would be scary for Jack about not trying?"

"Well, he'd worry that he might fail."

"Ah . . . so if Jack is not stressed enough, he might be afraid that he's not trying hard enough and fail."

"Exactly."

"Okay, I hear you. What then would *that* be like for Jack? To not try hard enough and fail?"

"That would be the worst. I can't imagine failing. I want to go to Tulane, and if I fail I can kiss that goodbye." John so identified with Jack that he was able to bring the fear to himself.

"Okay, so for you if there was even a slight chance that you'd not put yourself under enough stress, you might be risking your chance at getting into Tulane, something you've dreamed of achieving your whole life?"

"Yeah . . . yeah."

"Hmm . . . well, this is starting to make sense. I mean it makes perfect sense to me now. So for you, right now it is kind of like 'I need to be as far away from under no stress as I can be so that I don't even come close to risking losing my dream.'"

John nods.

"So over here" (pointing to *no stress*), "you risk failure; I wonder what you're risking over here" (pointing to *too much stress*).

"I don't think I'm risking anything over there."

"Really, then why are you here?"

"Because I'm having panic attacks and can't sleep and can't focus."

"That's right."

Is it clear to you what's causing those symptoms for John? He has chronic, extreme stress. It's clear to John as well. A kid like this is bright, and as I said, he's self-aware, so he's going to make that connection. If I had asked the next question in a too leading a way or made it obvious to him that he's causing his own problem, he'd resent me for it (unconscious at first but eventually he'd dislike that I did that to him). *Everyone, teens included, want to be the expert on their own life.* Period. When you step into the "expert" position on their problem, life, or situation, it stings. It's important to let John save face.

So I switched the subject and let some time pass before I drew the session to a close. This was a good time for appropriate self-disclosure, so I shared from my own experience: "God, I hate having panic attacks. I mean, I've learned how to manage them now, at forty-five years old, but when I was your age, I was at their mercy. It was like I couldn't breathe and that would make me panic even more. What are yours like?" He described similar symptoms, and we both agreed that panic attacks suck.

After enough time had gone by that we'd safely left the stress-anxiety relationship behind, I looked at the board and said, "Hmm . . . you know—hold on—I don't know here, but . . ." I got up and wrote the words "panic attacks" and "anxiety" on the board. Then I individually circled the words "stress," "too much stress," "no stress," "panic attacks," and "anxiety." "I guess we got all this stuff. As I look at this, it just looks overwhelming, huh?"

"Yeah, it sure does."

"It can just kind of all blend together."

"Exactly. And that's when I get overwhelmed."

John hit on an important point, showing why it's so important for us to understand and be educated about these matters. When we are able to name what we're feeling, what we're experiencing, and can begin to understand the relationship between seemingly unrelated problems, experiences, and symptoms, we gain a sense of control over them. It's like when you feel terrible enough to go to the doctor when you don't know what's wrong and within minutes the doctor says, "You have the flu." As bad as we feel physically, we feel better emotionally because we now understand *why* we're experiencing what we're experiencing.

I asked John, "As you look at this board, all this stuff is there, any way any of these things are related? I don't know if they are or aren't, but I guess I'm just wondering." I wasn't being dishonest with John. The reality is that these things are only related when *he* can relate them. And I've seen the exception to every rule.

"Well"—John started, before I interrupted (intentionally).

"Hold on." I handed him a different color marker. "Show me. If there's any connection there at all, just draw it for me." This is a powerful tool to help teens own their experience, and it gives him *full* control over making any and all connections.

He drew lines connecting all the circles. I asked, "Okay, so I see they're connected. Is there any relationship among them?"

He then drew double lines between stress and anxiety and panic attacks. "Wow. Okay," I said.

He went on to describe how chronic extreme stress, driven by fear of failure, was causing him problems on the other end. "So I guess I have to decide which feels worse, the panic attacks or the failure."

"Maybe. But how does failure feel?"

"Bad."

"When did you fail?" I asked.

"Well, I didn't yet, but it would feel terrible."

"So for you is it kinda like I'd rather deal with the pain I have and *know* rather than face the pain of failure, which is unknown and could be even worse than the anxiety?"

"Yeah."

John eventually, slowly, learned to moderate his stress. A kid like John, unbeknownst to him, can't be stress free. He doesn't have it in his DNA. He's not hardwired like that. Long before he gets to failure, the breaker will kick off to protect him from that. For him, and for many other perfectionistic teens, the problem is that right now the breaker is tripping way too early, driving him in the other direction.

WHAT IS STRESS?

Stress can simply be the painful feeling you experience when you *perceive* that you are unable to meet expectations. The key word for stress is "perception." The objective reality may or may not be true, but if you perceive you can't meet the expectations placed on you, by yourself, others, the world, or God, you will experience stress.

Believe it or not, there is such a thing as good stress. Good stress has these characteristics:

• It's episodic or brief.
• It channels energy and focuses efforts.
• It is perceived as able to lead one to growth and expanded opportunities.

- It can feel good, motivating, or even exciting (and even occur alongside feelings of nervousness).

An example of good stress would be physical exercise. When you walk, run, or lift weights, you are putting your muscles in a state of good stress. Your muscles literally expand and grow in response to that stress. There is also good emotional stress. For instance, when you have to prepare for an event, be it an exam, a dinner party, or even a lesson plan, you can experience good stress. In each of these instances you have an opportunity to grow, make the best use of your time and energy, and perhaps learn how to do each of these tasks more efficiently.

You might be thinking, *Roy, I've had those experiences and they were far from good! I get panic attacks when I'm in those situations!* And there's the worst part about stress: often, not always, *whether we experience a stressful event as good or bad depends on how we process the stressful event.* That's right, most stressful events can be either good or bad depending on how we look at the experience.

For example, my family and I are in the car at a fast-food drive-through and the line is wrapped twice around the building. For my family, this creates positive anticipation. They begin talking about what they want to order and read it as a sign that what we're about to eat is going to be amazing. I mean it must be if this many people are waiting for it, right? For me? I get frustrated and wonder how one of the most efficient fast-food franchises in the world could be more efficient and "Why is it taking so long? I'm hungry!" This causes me to contract, both literally and figuratively. If you were to watch me, I begin hunching over, sighing because I'm trying to take deep breaths to calm myself, and complaining out loud to my family who can do nothing about it. This is the same event, but the type of stress depends on how it's interpreted.

Stress can direct us toward positive experiences or outcomes in our lives. Good stress is a useful tool. It's built into not only our DNA but also the Catholic liturgical year. For two seasons of the Church year we intentionally put stress into our lives.

During Advent, a time of anticipation and preparation for the coming of Jesus, we experience the stress of waiting, of delaying

immediate gratification as we recall the waiting done by our spiritual ancestors in the dessert. And we dig into the stress of waiting and
watching for Christ's presence in our lives every day and in fullness
at the end of time. During Lent, we willingly add stress to our lives
by taking on the three spiritual disciplines of fasting, almsgiving,
and prayer.

WHAT IS UNHEALTHY STRESS?

Unhealthy stress is any type of stress that we are unable to cope with
in a healthy way. Unhealthy stress has the following characteristics:

- causes anxiety or severe worrying;
- feels wholly unpleasant (no part of it feels good or exciting);
- negatively affects performance and behavior;
- can lead to mental or physical problems; and
- can be episodic and brief or long term.

There are plenty of bad stressors out there, and our teens know them
too well. For many, negative stress is a result of events or expectations
that occur in their lives. Often, young people have little to no control
over some of these events. For example, Jaime, whose parents were
pursuing a divorce, shared: "I didn't choose this. My life was going
along just fine, Roy, until these two decided to rip our [bleeping] lives
apart. Thanks for the gift, as if I didn't already have enough on my
plate, Mom and Dad!"

For Gabby, going through a tornado when she was a kid caused
her stress: "It was like everything was going crazy. You heard the
horns go off and then the hail began slamming into the house. Daddy
dragged me into the storm cellar. When we came out, everyone was
crying and everything was destroyed." Like divorce, the trauma of
natural disasters has serious and potentially long-term effects on
young people. The following examples reveal additional triggers of
bad stress common for teens.

Social Media

In a counseling session with Jessica, a seventeen-year-old high school junior, she said, "You know, even we know it's affecting us. We may not want to admit it, but we know always being on our phones is not good for us, but it's kind of like an addiction; you know it's bad for you but you can't stop."

Jessica wasn't exactly sure in what specific ways social media was bad for her friends and her, but she did know they weren't really happy. When pressed to pay attention to her moods while on Snapchat or Instagram, she said, "I was so anxious. I never realized that before. It's not like anything was bad, just I kept waiting to see something that would upset me. It didn't happen, but I was still worried about it. Even after I got off."

I asked, "What would upset you?"

"Well, you know . . . like if I saw some of my friends get together without me. Or an ex with another girl. Sometimes it's that my friends get to do something, but because my parents are so strict, I don't get to do those things." For every teen like Jessica, I've heard at least twenty others express similar sentiments. Social media stresses teens out in a number of ways.

Fear of Missing Out (FOMO)

Even when teens are not comparing themselves to others, a constant stream of watching what others are doing can make us feel we are missing out on something even when we're not sure what that is or might be. This doesn't just affect teens. Pay attention to your mood and thoughts next time you are on social media. I often find that my mood is affected when I scroll through my Facebook or Instagram feed. I'm prone to get jealous and get down when comparing myself to others. That's a quite common experience and, left unchecked, can become a problem.

A Potential Waste of Time

There are certainly times when teens need a low-energy mental task, and the thought of catching up with their friends can be refreshing.

But social media and other online pursuits can subtly suck them into "zoning out" and losing track of how much time they're spending. Even teens don't feel good about themselves when they know they're wasting time and there are other important tasks or projects that need their time and attention.

Doesn't Meet Their Need for Intimacy

What young people deeply crave, and what social media promises but underdelivers, is connection. It feels like a connection, but it's not the intimacy and closeness they really want. Social media and other technologies may add to an already-existing connection and help it to continue in the absence of the ability to be face-to-face. But it cannot replace our need for real-time, face-to-face, in-person human interaction. As one teen said, "I'll get on hoping to feel better but get off feeling even more disconnected and scattered than I was before. But I keep going back. It's like an abusive relationship I guess."

Political Climate

There has been an increasing lack of civility in public discourse in recent years. Presidential and other national elections have proved to be mean-spirited and filled with personal attacks. There is much vitriol rather than healthy, spirited debates about ideas and the future of our country and world.

I met with one young teen who was having panic attacks after watching the presidential debates in 2016. "They just kept yelling at each other. I have to hear that all the time with my parents; it was just too much to have to watch it on TV as well."

Media

Media outlets make advertising dollars by attracting viewers to their content. Good news doesn't sell, but bad news does: "If no one bleeds, no one reads." Accurate, real-time stories on their own don't draw nearly as much attention as sensationalized, exaggerated accounts.

Add to that the twenty-four-hour, nonstop news cycle with countless outlets to receive real-time news and commentary and teens can be exposed to sensationalized, often-dramatized narratives of events and situations that may not even be accurate.

The way that acts of terror, violence, and suffering in our world today are reported has increased the stress, fears, and anxiety of many teens. Teens need to feel safe, despite their words and actions that indicate otherwise. I've seen many teens who shrug off acts of terrorism at first but, when probed a little deeper, reveal they are scared and feel powerless and sad.

Family Issues

As we read earlier, the "traditional" family as once understood barely exists today in the United States (see pages 6–10). It's estimated that less than 7 percent of US families meet that description. The absolute majority of young people today live in "nontraditional" families, which as we mentioned earlier can put them at risk for experiencing unhealthy stress, anxiety, and depression.

Divorcing Religion

An increasing number of families today are divorcing religion and in some cases God altogether. In surveys of religious affiliation, the largest group today is "unaffiliated." This ever-growing group of Americans who choose not to affiliate with any particular religion or denomination aren't necessarily atheists or agnostics. They just don't want to participate in organized religion. Religious practice helps teens to deal with stress, step back from it, put it in greater perspective, and find healthier ways of relating to it.

Busyness

Young people today are busy. The word "busy" should almost be included in the definition of the world "teenager." The availability of activities, alongside increased cultural pressures to do it all and have it all, is making young lives overpacked with appointments, tutors, private lessons, games, practices, rehearsals, recitals, tournaments, and so forth. There's a sense from parents that in order for their child to grow up and be healthy and successful, they must be allowed and even encouraged to participate in everything possible. As one parent so poignantly said to me, "If I don't allow her to participate in all of these activities, then she won't have a shot at getting into a good college, which we know means everything to her future." Many youth have accepted that last statement as fact and in turn, like their parents and an increasing number of other adults, have adopted—albeit in many cases unconsciously—a definition of success that drives one to overwork and underrest. Many youth and their families have come to overvalue academic and extracurricular achievement at the expense of healthy, well-tended relationships.

This definition of success is not informed by the Gospel. Nowhere in the Bible will you find anything to support academic, athletic, social, or financial success as the path to happiness. In fact, you'll find the opposite. Jesus says to the young man, "If you wish to be perfect, go sell what you have and give to the poor. . . . Then come, follow me" (Mt 19:21). Ironically, this is what so many young people and their families are striving for: perfection. Yet it is a very limited, Western understanding of perfection that is unattainable in this life. Helping young people see this and understand it is a major goal of accompanying them.

SYNONYMS OF STRESS

Often young people will tell you when they are stressed. "I'm just so stressed out!" might be the most repeated phrase I've ever heard working with young people. Yet often enough they *won't* use the word "stress" but instead use other descriptors. It's important to know the synonyms of and phrases related to stress so we are able to recognize it. Here are a few:

- overwhelmed
- overloaded
- it's just too much (to handle)

- I can't take the pressure
- pressure cooker
- freaking out
- grrrr

The problem with these words and phrases is that teens will just as often use them to describe situations that are inherently positive stressors as they will for unhealthy stressors. But when we're aware of the language they use to describe their experiences, we have an opportunity to discuss it with them to better assess whether they are in a healthy or unhealthy stressful situation.

KEY POINTS

- Many teens today are under tremendous amounts of stress related to succeeding in school, which leads to chronic anxiety.
- Stress can be defined as the experience of perceiving that you are unable to meet expectations.
- Good stress is that which makes our muscles—spiritual, physical, or emotional—stronger when they are needed to respond.
- Teens are affected by many of the same stressors that adults face but will respond to them differently than adults.
- Social media is a significant source of stress for many teens. It can cause young people to feel like they're missing out on social experiences and to waste their time, and it fails to meet their needs for intimacy.
- Other sources of stress for young people today include the political climate, media, family issues, and being too busy.
- It is critical to understand the difference between good and bad stress and to be able to recognize those differences within our own lives and those of young people.
- Teens will use various synonyms for stress, including "overwhelmed," "pressure cooker," and "freaking out."

ASK YOURSELF

Spend a few moments making a list with two columns, one for the significant sources of stress in your life and another for how you respond to those stressors. Then consider the following:

1. Did making this list of my stressors and my responses to them help me feel better in any way? In what ways?
2. Do I feel this activity would be helpful to a young person struggling with stress?
3. Can I see myself going through this exercise with young people?
4. After reading this chapter, do I have a better understanding of how stress can lead to anxiety and depression?

FOR INSPIRATION AND PRAYER

Nebuchadnezzar's face became livid with utter rage against Shadrach, Meshach, and Abednego. He ordered the furnace to be heated seven times more than usual and had some of the strongest men in his army bind Shadrach, Meshach, and Abednego and cast them into the white-hot furnace. They were bound and cast into the white-hot furnace with their trousers, shirts, hats and other garments, for the king's order was urgent. So huge a fire was kindled in the furnace that the flames devoured the men who threw Shadrach, Meshach, and Abednego into it. But these three fell, bound, into the midst of the white-hot furnace. They walked about in the flames, singing to God and blessing the Lord. . . .

The flames rose forty-nine cubits above the furnace, and spread out, burning the Chaldeans that it caught around the furnace. But the angel of the Lord went down into the furnace with Azariah and his companions, drove the fiery flames out of the furnace, and made the inside of the furnace as though a dew-laden breeze were blowing through it. The fire in no way touched them or caused them pain or harm. Then these three in the furnace with one voice sang, glorifying and blessing God.

—Daniel 3:19–24, 47–51

When the disciples saw him walking on the sea they were terrified. "It is a ghost," they said, and they cried out in fear. At once [Jesus] spoke to them, "Take courage, it is I; do not be afraid." Peter said to him in reply, "Lord, if it is you, command me to come to you on the water." He said, "Come." Peter got out of the boat and began to walk on the water toward Jesus. But when he saw how [strong] the wind was he became frightened; and, beginning to sink, he cried out, "Lord, save me!" Immediately Jesus stretched out his hand and caught him, and said to him, "O you of little faith, why did you doubt?"

—Matthew 14:26–31

Peace I leave with you; my peace I give to you. Not as the world gives do I give it to you. Do not let your hearts be troubled or afraid.

—John 14:27

5. RECOGNIZING ANXIETY AND DEPRESSION

Tate did everything right: had good behavior, got perfect grades, and excelled at several sports. When I met with his parents, after twenty minutes of telling me how great a kid he was, Tate's dad said in perfect Cajun English, "Something ain't right, Mistuh Roy. It's jus' dat he ain't happy no moh."

"What makes you say that, Mr. Elaire?" I asked. Tate's mom continued to let her husband speak. The parents interacted like many Cajun couples where old patriarchal roles dictate that men do the talking when it is important business.

"He don' smile; he always in his room. And, mais, his *grades* are droppin'. Das not him, Mistuh Roy!" Tate's dad said loudly, exasperated, forcing himself to hold back the tears of confusion and fear that were welling up. "Dis kid's smart, Mistuh Roy!"

"I wonder where he got that from," I said, smiling.

"His mamma, tank you, Jesus. She got all duh brains, Mistuh Roy. She even went to college."

"Okay, so if I'm hearing you right, is it kind of like, 'Man, I'm so worried about my boy, cause he ain't actin' normal and I'm worried that he'll mess up his future if he don't get his stuff together with his grades'?" I asked.

"Exactly, Mistuh Roy. He got a real future. I don toll him thousands of times, 'Tate, you don' wanna work in duh Gulf, bruh. It's hard out dare, workin' on dem rigs. I been lucky, but at any moment things could change. You got opportunities I never had.'" He stopped short because he was forcing himself not to cry. As he talked, Mr. Elaire was beginning to realize something that was important to him as a dad, to make sure his kid had a better shot at having a better life than he had. And he had succeeded, but now something was threatening what he had spent his life working for.

"I hear you, my brother. I hear you. You've been busting your butt all these years to give him an opportunity, one you never got, but you wanna make damn sure he has it and that he takes advantage of it."

"Yes, sir. You got it." He turned to his wife. "We in duh right place, Cecile," he said.

I did nothing but listen. This man had complete faith in me simply because I spent a few minutes really trying to understand him and listened to him.

"So, what else can you tell me about Tate?" I asked.

"I dunno, Mistuh Roy. Das it I think," he said, then looking at his wife, "Mamma, whach you tink?"

"Yes, Ms. Cecile, I'd really like to know what you've seen."

"Well, Doctuh Rah, dis all started about nine months ago."

Bingo, I think, because kids like this rarely just wake up depressed. There are many factors that contribute to anxiety and depression, some of them physiological, and we now know you can be predisposed genetically to become depressed. But this kid was fine for sixteen years.

"Do you know of anything that happened in the last couple years that would have negatively affected Tate?"

"Not really, but he changed," his mother continued. "Das when he began stayin' in his room all the time, he stopped eatin' his rice and gravy, and he slept all duh time."

"And how long has this been going on?" I asked.

"Almos' a year, I guess."

Ideally, Tate's parents would have brought him to me eight months sooner, as the earlier you can address most mental health issues, the better. But they didn't know that those symptoms, classic symptoms of depression, when they persist for more than two weeks, often indicate a serious emotional problem that needs attention from a counselor or other mental health professional.

RECOGNIZING THE SIGNS

Tate's parents are not alone. They join millions of other parents each year who don't recognize the warning signs of depression and anxiety or who don't know what to do about it if they do see these signs.

WHAT IS DEPRESSION?

According to the National Institute of Mental Health (NIMH), depression is a common but serious mood disorder that can cause severe symptoms affecting how you feel, think, and handle daily activities such as sleeping, eating, and working.[1] If these symptoms persist for at least two weeks, depression is a likely reason.

As explored in chapter 1, the US Department of Health and Human Services reports that one out of every eight adolescents will experience a depressive episode, which is a bout of depression lasting longer than two weeks, but at some point the symptoms will subside.[2]

What Are the Warning Signs or Symptoms of Depression?

Later in this chapter we will explore how to watch for and respond to signs of depression, but for now, let's see what they are. The NIMH lists the following as common symptoms of depression:

- persistent sad, anxious, or "empty" mood
- feelings of hopelessness, or pessimism
- irritability
- feelings of guilt, worthlessness, or helplessness
- loss of interest or pleasure in hobbies and activities
- decreased energy or fatigue
- moving or talking more slowly
- feeling restless or having trouble sitting still
- difficulty concentrating, remembering, or making decisions
- difficulty sleeping, early morning awakening, or oversleeping

- appetite and/or weight changes
- thoughts of death or suicide, or suicide attempts
- aches or pains, headaches, cramps, or digestive problems without a clear physical cause and/or that do not ease with treatment[3]

A few not mentioned by the NIMH but that show up in youth and teens are:

- falling grades
- inability to focus
- friends asking if something's wrong
- teachers, coaches, and other adults asking if something's wrong (both are indicative of adults being concerned but not wanting to assume there's a problem)
- rage
- substance abuse
- legal problems
- discipline problems at school
- not wanting to go to school

WHAT IS ANXIETY?

It's normal to feel anxious periodically. But young people with an anxiety disorder experience more than just normal worries or fears. They will often experience similar fears much more intensely and experience them more consistently—even constantly—compared to teens with the expected occasional anxiety that eventually subsides.

When I had first met with Ashley, she was stiff on my couch. But not the "uncomfortable" kind of stiff. She was the kind of stiff that I've come to recognize as a symptom of an overactive fight/flight mechanism often affecting teens with chronic anxiety.

Ashley said, "I always worry something bad's gonna happen."

"And by 'always' you mean . . . ?" I asked.

"All the time," she said. "I'm worried about my grades, school, friends, my parents' financial situation."

"Wow, that's a lot of worrying!" I said.

"Yeah and my stomach is always hurting. I even throw up when I get too worried, and now I'm not leaving the house because I never know when and where I'll throw up."

Ashley had begun avoiding going places because she was worried about throwing up in public. She is one of the millions of young people whose anxiety is so bad, it has physical symptoms.

What Does Anxiety Look Like?

- irritability
- difficulty falling asleep
- self-injury
- depression/suicidal thoughts
- apathy
- dishonesty
- obsessions
- counting random things such as steps and ceiling tiles
- handwashing
- lock checking
- needing constant reassurance
- perfectionism

What Are the Different Types of Anxiety?

In addition to knowing behaviors that may be signs of an anxiety disorder, it will help for you to be familiar with the most common types of anxiety experienced by young people.

Generalized Anxiety Disorder (GAD)

GAD is characterized by excessive worry about family issues, relationships, grades, peers, sports, and other extracurricular performance.

Obsessive-Compulsive Disorder (OCD)

Technically, OCD is no longer an anxiety disorder, but many teens who have any type of anxiety have what I call "OCD-like" symptoms.

OCD is characterized by unwanted or intrusive thoughts (obsessions) and a feeling of being compelled to repeatedly perform rituals (compulsions) as a way of trying to cope with the anxiety. You might hear some adolescents say they have "pure O." This means, they don't have the physical compulsions, such as checking locks, handwashing, having to trace their fingers around certain objects, or doing things in a certain order with exact precision every time. Rather, these individuals have more cognitive compulsions, such as counting ceiling tiles or having to follow thoughts that are being rapidly generated, which can split off into other thoughts in a seemingly endless expansion of splintering thoughts. In the words of one young woman, "It's like each of my thoughts is a blade on a ceiling fan, but after a while each blade spins off and becomes a new fan with more blades."

Panic Disorder

Panic disorder is generally defined as a young person experiencing two or more panic or anxiety attacks, followed by at least one month worrying about having another panic attack.

Post-Traumatic Stress Disorder (PTSD)

This type of anxiety disorder afflicts individuals who have experienced a traumatic event and subsequently have intense fears and anxiety. Youth can become emotionally numb and easily irritated, and they might avoid certain people, places, or types of experiences. Not every child who experiences traumatic events develops PTSD. It's important for adults to realize that trauma is in the eye of the beholder. This means that what might be traumatic for one youth may not be traumatic for another. What makes an event traumatic differs for each individual but is usually a combination of inner resources such as temperament and self-awareness, good habits such as physical exercise, and outer resources such as supportive friends and adults who can help them make sense of and manage a significant traumatic event. Because trauma depends on how people respond to a particular event at a particular time in their lives, two teens can experience the same event, such as the death of a classmate to whom they were both close, yet one is traumatized and the other is not. One teen uses a healthy support network of friends, family, and other caring adults who help her process the event, while the other closes off to and isolates himself from those who could offer compassion and support.

Separation Anxiety Disorder

This is usually experienced in youth between the ages of seven and nine but also occurs in a small percentage of teenagers. These young people experience excessive anxiety when away from home or separated from parents or caregivers.

Social Anxiety Disorder (SAD)

SAD is characterized by an intense fear of social and performance situations and activities such as going into the lunchroom, participating in an activity, and starting conversations with peers (both known and unknown). I'm seeing more and more social anxiety disorder among Generation Z kids for whom virtual communication is very comfortable but their excessive virtual lives often exclude time for in-person, face-to-face interactions. Because of this, many young people are becoming less proficient at face-to-face interactions and conversations and end up feeling a great deal of anxiety when faced with such situations.

   As you read through the warning signs and symptoms of anxiety and depression, you might think that many of them could in fact be "symptoms" of adolescence. And you'd be correct. So how do you know when a behavior or symptom falls under the category of normal or is an indicator of disorder?

NORMAL VERSUS ABNORMAL BEHAVIOR

It's normal for teens to become surly, withdrawn, and—let's be honest—obnoxious. But how can you tell if a teen is being a "typical teenager" or showing the warning signs of anxiety and depression? How can you distinguish typical teenage behavior from dangerous red flags?

Appearance

Normal

Fashions are constantly changing, and it's important to teens to keep up with these changes. It's also important for them to do two things simultaneously: be included and stand out. With their appearance they want to be in style while maintaining their own look. Today's teenagers want tattoos and piercings more than any previous generation. It's their way of standing out and fitting in. Parents will of course differ on allowing piercings and tattoos, but it's important to know that the desire for them and attempts to get them are normal.

Abnormal

Sudden, drastic changes of appearance, especially when a teen is experiencing social or school-related problems, or self-harm behaviors such as cutting are not normal, and these behaviors need immediate professional attention. Any sudden or extreme weight loss or gain is also a red flag that warrants professional help.

Rebelliousness

Normal

As teenagers grow, so does their capacity for abstract thought. Combine that newfound ability to think critically with a drive to become their own persons and you've got the source of a lot of what stresses adults who care about them. Being argumentative, inquisitive, skeptical, questioning, doubting, and disobedient are all normal teenage behaviors and should be expected—*no matter how well they've been raised or how good they are.*

Abnormal

Teenagers who are too good, too nice, or too consistently acquiescent concern me and potentially indicate an unhealthy need to please or excessive anxiety about making mistakes. On the other hand, constant and consistent escalation of arguments at home or at school, violence, skipping school, and legal problems are all concerning behaviors as well and merit careful observation and some kind of intervention.

Mood

Normal

The developing teenage brain is like a buzzing beehive. A whole lot is going on in there. Hormone generation and regulation as well as a host of other processes to help them integrate their personalities, make sense of their lives, survive in the world, and find meaning make it difficult for teens to maintain the stability of mood commonly expected and seen in adults. Going from being happy or joyful to being sad, worried, preoccupied, irritable, and angry are all normal for the developing teen.

Abnormal

Mood swings that are unusually intense or rapid or that happen consistently and sudden changes in a teenager's personality are not normal. Pay attention to a change in schoolwork. Falling grades, especially sudden falling grades, when they cannot be otherwise explained, are usually a cause for concern. Changes in sleep patterns, inability to fall or stay asleep, should be discussed. Any mention of suicide should be taken seriously. Even if the teen isn't a threat to themselves, it may indicate underlying depression, a desperate need for attention, inability to cope with circumstances, and their accompanying emotions. Any sudden or drastic change in routine should be noted and possibly discussed.

Substances

Normal

Most teens want to or do experiment with drugs, alcohol, or tobacco/nicotine products. It's important to have open, forthright discussions about what substances really do to the teen brain. In addition to using the latest scientific research about how substances affect their brain, adults should also discuss values, expectations, and consequences for abusing substances.

Abnormal

Any habitual use of substances is something needing more attention. As I've said before, any of these abnormal behaviors when combined with other problems at home, at school, or in their social lives warrant more concern.

Socially

Normal

As teens grow they will be less influenced by parents and more influenced by their peers and other caring adults. While they live at home, school and their friendships are, for teens, a second home and family. This normal withdrawing of teens is often painful and worrisome for parents. If you're a parent, discuss this with your teen, but understand that this is a normal teenage behavior. If you teach or minister with teens, be alert to this shifting dynamic, and when possible, use your influence to help the teen grow in empathy for how this healthy and necessary process affects others who care about them.

Abnormal

If a teen suddenly or drastically changes friends or friend groups without sufficient explanation, this is a cause for concern. If teenagers' friends are influencing them to do anything illegal, if teens are blatantly disobedient to reasonable rules and expectations, and if they refuse to comply with consequences for their behavior, there is cause for heightened concern.

Spiritual

Normal

It's normal for teens to question their faith, doubt the existence of God, and be skeptical and questioning of religious leaders and institutions. Not only is this normal, but also, when they receive support from adults during this process, this "kicking against the goad" is quite healthy in the formation of faith, spirituality, and a life ethic that the teenager owns, rather than one they ascribe to out of obligation.

Abnormal

Sudden changes of beliefs, refusal to attend family church services, and fear of attending church services especially when accompanied by other problems in different areas of their life are warning signs that should be heeded. There are ways to talk with teens about any changes in their beliefs or attitudes toward God, religion, or religious institutions. And while the tools of chapter 7 on listening will help immensely, here are a few tips for addressing the issue of teens not believing in God or pushing back against the Church:

1. Don't panic. As important as your faith is to you and as badly as you want teens to integrate that faith into their lives, it is not urgent, nor is it an emergency. Overreacting and panicking about this issue will cause teens to dismiss any help you may be able to offer.

2. Ask questions, listen, and check with them to make sure you understand what they are saying. You don't need to persuade, cajole, or otherwise force teens to believe in God or in Church teachings. If you do, they will resist, and you're wasting your time. Ask them genuinely curious questions and listen to their responses. Then go back and tell them what you heard to make sure you really understand. This will validate them as a person, not give them permission to leave the Church.

3. Sudden shifts in religious belief or behavior are often the result of a changing peer group or a negative experience that teens wish God had protected them from. They could also be because of a scandalous act they heard about or witnessed or a negative experience with a faith leader. When these issues surface, which they will if you listen well, you have an opportunity to discuss those issues, which is what the teen really needs.

WHAT CAN ADULTS DO TO HELP?

It's critical to be aware of the signs and symptoms of stress. But you're reading this because you want to help. This book is full of practical tips for helping teens, but it can be as simple as looking, listening, and asking.

Listen

Teens are constantly communicating with adults, but too often we're distracted, not ever paying *full* attention. Teens know this and will not tell us the *most* important concerns on their minds and hearts if we're not fully tuned in. Listen, listen, and listen even more. Ask questions for clarification. Admit you're being annoying but tell them that it's important to you to really understand: "Look, I know I'm a nag, and I'll leave you alone if that's what you really want, even though I really don't think it is, but I do want to understand what you're going through. You say 'nuthin' but everything in me says 'somethin'!"

Look

Are there drastic changes in attitudes, grades, friends, social activities, and other behaviors? Are there *consistent* eruptions of anger? Does the *intensity* of the teen's reaction consistently not match the level of what triggered the reaction? Are there *sudden*, drastic changes in appearance, weight, or style?

Ask

It has always taken a village to raise teenagers, but today very few live in the village. We must intentionally re-create the village. Ask teachers, ministers, friends of the teen you are concerned about, parents, your friends who share your values, experts, and anyone else who knows the teenager or will listen to you if they think what you're seeing is normal or if it is a problem. Look for what's consistent in their verbal responses and facial expressions when you describe the behaviors or changes that concern you. If you've determined there is a problem, it's time to ask for help. Ask people whose discretion you trust, if they can recommend any professionals who might help you to determine the severity of the problem and what you can do to help.

KEY POINTS

- Depression is a common but serious mood disorder that affects how you feel, think, and handle daily activities such as sleeping, eating, or working for at least two weeks. At times symptoms are mild, but they can also be severe.
- Adults who want to help young people today cannot effectively do so without recognizing the many symptoms of depression. Many youth don't even know they are depressed, and an adult who recognizes the signs may be the key to healing.
- Young people with anxiety disorders experience more than just normal worries or fears. They will often experience similar fears much more intensely or experience them more consistently or constantly as opposed to normal occasional anxiety that eventually subsides.
- There are various signs of anxiety in young people, including irritability, self-injury, and depression.
- There are also multiple types of anxiety disorders experienced by young people; these disorders include social anxiety disorder, panic disorder, and obsessive-compulsive disorder.

- Adults who want to work with young people must be aware of the various signs and types of anxiety and anxiety disorders to offer youth the best assistance possible.
- Indicators of abnormal behavior in teens include sudden changes in appearance, mood, or social groups; abuse of substances; rebelliousness; and changes in spiritual life.
- Adults can help teens struggling with stress and anxiety disorders by attentively and compassionately listening to teens; looking for signs of sudden changes in behavior, attitude, or appearance; and asking other adults for guidance and support.

ASK YOURSELF

1. How many of the signs of anxiety and depression in young people do I find in my own experiences as an adult or when I was a young person?
2. If I have struggled with anxiety or depression, or any of the disorders discussed in this chapter, how did or do I cope? What strategies and people do I rely on as I seek healing?
3. What are some reasons that adults miss or misunderstand the signs of anxiety and depression in young people today?
4. How can I become involved with creating a "takes a village" culture among adults who work with young people in my locale?

FOR INSPIRATION AND PRAYER

Do not neglect to do good and to share what you have; God is pleased by sacrifices of that kind.
—Hebrews 13:16

This is my commandment: love one another as I love you. No one has greater love than this, to lay down one's life for one's friends. You are my friends if you do what I command you. I no longer call you slaves, because a slave does not know what his master is doing. I have called you

friends, because I have told you everything I have heard from my Father. It was not you who chose me, but I who chose you and appointed you to go and bear fruit that will remain, so that whatever you ask the Father in my name he may give you. This I command you: love one another.
—John 15:12–17

Do not withhold any goods from the owner
    when it is in your power to act.
—Proverbs 3:27

Rejoice with those who rejoice, weep with those who weep.
—Romans 12:15

6. AVOIDING THE UNDUE PRESSURES OF SUCCESS

Allie, a sixteen-year-old high school sophomore, approached me after I spoke at her school's general assembly on anxiety and depression. She was the president of the student body and had held multiple leadership positions in other school organizations and activities. Her parents were both successful.

"What you said made so much sense to me, Mr. Roy," she said. "So what can I do about my anxiety? I mean, I need to do something about this."

"I agree. What do you want to do about it?" I asked.

"I dunno, but I wanna fix it," she said in a determined voice, hoping to handle anxiety much like any of the projects and tasks she already ran so well.

"What do you wanna fix?" I asked again.

"My anxiety," she said, frustrated and with a facial expression indicating *What else idiot?*

"Okay, so what do you think's causing your anxiety?"

"I dunno."

"Okay, I only ask because after working with many teens over the years, I've learned that if I help you get rid of your anxiety too quickly without you or me first figuring out how it got there, it won't work. It may surprise you to know that many people, even after figuring out what causes it, really don't want to get rid of their anxiety. Sometimes they discover that it helps them get things done. And you strike me as someone who likes to get things done. I know that because there are a thousand other kids up there and about 30 percent of them have anxiety, but you're the only one down here right now wanting to do something about it. Good for you."

"Hmm." She thought for a moment. "Now that I think about it, you're right. It does help."

"In what way?" I asked.

"Well, it drives me, I guess."

"How so?"

"Well, when I worry that I'm about to make a mistake or mess something up, I can kick myself into another gear."

"What happens when you get in that gear?"

"I get stuff done. A lot done." She smiled, revealing how much she liked getting things done.

"I hear ya; I like to get stuff done too. I *really* like it."

We both laughed as she felt we were alike in some way.

"But I guess the real question is, what does it mean for you to make a mistake?" I asked.

"I mean, I've failed. And failure is not an option," she said.

"What will happen if you fail? Will your parents get mad at you?" I asked.

"Oh no, not at all," she said. "I think they'd be happy if I made a B, or messed up a little."

"Really?" I asked in disbelief, assuming that her parents exerted pressure for her to achieve her potential.

"Yeah, they think I'm too hard on myself. They're always telling me to 'lighten up.'" She continued, "But I want to be successful, and I know that in order to do that I've got to work hard."

"When you say 'successful,' what does that mean for you?" I asked.

"I mean, you know, what it means to everybody here: get into a good college so I can get a good job."

"Oh. Is that all it means?" I asked.

"Well, I want to be happy. But I can't see myself being happy without getting a good job and making good money."

I was beginning to learn that Allie, like a growing number of young people today, had not spent much time thinking about what success would really look like for her. For Allie, success was a destination to be reached. She would know she reached her destination when she finally got a "good" job, whatever that meant, and made "good money," whatever that meant. She, like many others, assumed these things would make her happy. But you, like me, probably know many people who have "good" jobs and make "good" money. Yet they would describe their lives as being far from happy. If good jobs and good money were the secret to happiness, celebrities, millionaires, and billionaires wouldn't be taking their own lives every day.

WHAT WE WANT VERSUS WHAT WE MOST DEEPLY WANT

The late American psychiatrist Rollo May once said that we will only be truly happy when we are able to find a way to get beneath what we think we want and discover and pursue what we *most deeply* want.

What Allie would hopefully learn along the way is that a good job and good money *might*, but not necessarily, contribute to her happiness. If we'd had more time to visit, she might have come closer to discovering what she most deeply wanted, to be happy. Thomas Merton, a Trappist monk and renowned spiritual writer, reportedly once said, "People may spend their whole lives climbing the ladder of success only to find, once they reach the top, that the ladder is leaning against the wrong wall."

Success and happiness are important matters in the lives of young people, deserving critical thought and thorough discussion. Our role in this part of their development is crucial. We have the ability to help them consider what roles God, faith, community, and service play in their success and happiness. How can we help young people define "success" and "happiness" in ways that will allow them to live the kind of lives they most deeply desire?

THE DARK SIDE OF PERFECT

We're all familiar with the phrase from Matthew where Jesus exhorts us to "be perfect, just as your heavenly Father is perfect" (5:48). A fundamental misunderstanding of this scripture by an overly Western notion of perfection has caused many to be ruthless with themselves, demanding that they make no mistake in any area of their lives. For perfectionistic teens, making a small mistake is the gravest of sins. As one teen told me recently after making a small error causing him to make a 98 on a test, "I'm better than that. I should have aced it." Translation: I must be perfect. I'll accept nothing less from myself.

For many adults this conviction is also true. I once heard Fr. Ron Rolheiser, a systematic and spiritual theologian, explain that this is not the meaning of the Greek word *perfection*, so how ought we interpret this passage? The word used in the text is more accurately translated as *compassion* according to Rolheiser. I recall him saying that it would be more accurate to read, "Be compassionate as your heavenly father is compassionate." It is only when our compassion is perfect that we are in line with what God is asking us in this passage.

Anything in our lives that we want to change we must first acknowledge it, then accept it, and finally change it. (Name it. Claim it. Tame it.) For instance, when I was trying to lose weight, I lost a lot of it at first, but then that stopped. However, once I acknowledged that my obesity wasn't genetic but rather that I was a compulsive emotional overeater, I could break the plateau. When I began acknowledging that fact (named it) and accepting it (claimed it), then and only then could I begin working on the real problem (taming it). My obesity was a secondary problem to my emotional dysfunction.

THE POWER OF DENIAL

As a Cajun friend once joked, "Mais, duh-Nile ain't just a long river in Egypt." He was expressing how hard it is to overcome our natural instinct to avoid pain and seek pleasure. Young people don't wake up and say to themselves, "You know what? Today, I think I'm going to deny the fact that I've adopted an unhealthy definition of success." It happens slowly over time, and we are largely unaware of the many things we deny. For young people who are still growing in their ability to describe their experiences, denial is even easier.

HELPING YOUNG PEOPLE "GET REAL"

I'm always hearing teens say how they like it when people "get real" with them. What's challenging for them, which they seldom realize, is getting real with themselves.

Getting real means being authentic and being vulnerable with one's self. It means being honest about one's gifts and weaknesses. Getting real means admitting to one's self daily, "I'm not perfect. I'm not created to be perfect. But I can still do my best in a way that won't end up causing me harm in the long run."

This is area where adults play a critical role. Sometimes young people need us to help them see the reality. Depending on their age and maturity, they may only have a limited capacity to "get real" with themselves. A loving but challenging word from a parent or other caring adult can help them see outside themselves. For kids under ten years old, this is really hard to do on their own because their brains have not developed the ability to self-reflect or think about how they feel. In other words, while not impossible, it would be very difficult for a six-year-old to recognize that they have patterns of anxious thinking.

For preteens and teens, the process of individuating, becoming their own persons as distinct from their parents and other adult figures in their lives and even their own peers, has them often feeling as if they're on a stage before the whole world. They feel watched and often judged. To adults this looks like self-absorption, preoccupation with appearance, and even narcissism. These are all normal, but these inner stages make it hard for them to get real, to see what is really happening around them and inside themselves. We can do this in the following ways:

- Listening. When we listen to teens, we also help them listen to themselves. A teen can learn a lot about themselves while talking to a caring adult who actively listens to them. Chapter 8 is devoted to addressing the critical role of listening.
- Reflecting back to teens what you hear them saying. "So if I'm hearing you right, it sounds as if you're really confused about

whether or not to break up with your girlfriend? Am I understanding you correctly?"

- Asking permission to make an observation. It is far more effective to ask permission to make observations or offer advice than to just blurt it out. It honors the dignity of teens and gives them a chance to lower their own natural resistance to hear, evaluate, and then accept or reject your observation or advice.

PERFECTIONISM

An often-unrecognized form of anxiety is perfectionism. Here are a few examples of how perfectionism shows up in the lives of young people.

- The teens who get abnormally self-deprecating or sad at the first hint of a criticism.
- The teens who get depressed when they receive only 98 on a test and berates themselves, saying, "I should've gotten that one two-point question correct. I studied it for days!"
- The teens who are "people pleasers," constantly seeking the approval of others. (Yes, people pleasing can be a form of perfectionism.)
- The teens who know the answer, and even the teacher knows they know the answer, but won't raise their hand in class because they are afraid they'll get it wrong.
- The teens who quit sports they are really good at because they can't be the best at it.
- The teens who turn in assignments looking depressed, causing the teacher to think they are submitting subpar work when in reality the work is excellent.
- The teens who are always saying "I'm sorry" even when they've done nothing wrong.
- The teens who are always seeking reassurance that they're "good" and that they "did nothing wrong."
- The teens who have to do most things absolutely perfectly. (Somehow cleaning bedrooms so often escapes the need for perfection.)

- And for those who are Catholic, the teens who seem to be always going to confession. In religious circles this is often referred to as "scrupulosity."

In every single one of these examples, anxiety is the culprit. It may not seem like anxiety on the surface, but it is. Against a cultural backdrop where a growing number of teens are losing interest in academic achievement, getting their driver's licenses, and religious affiliation, a perfectionistic teen might seem heroic, even saintly! That's just one of the reasons perfectionistic anxiety is hard to identify, which makes it hard to treat as well.

Perfectionism is often not recognized as anxiety because it's been lauded for so long as the goal of healthy, Christian living. It's not hard to see how we've created a way for this type of anxiety to flourish in our culture. Consider the following:

- Matthew 5:48 says, "Be perfect, just as your heavenly Father is perfect," so what's wrong with striving for perfection? Instead of focusing on perfection, we should use this as an opportunity to talk about striving to be more compassionate and empathic with the needs and suffering of our brothers and sisters.
- Western notions of perfection are too often narrowed to meaning "without flaw." In contrast, in many parts of the world, "without flaw" is not a prerequisite for perfection and could disqualify something as being "perfect" because there is an deeper understanding that nothing in this life is without flaw.
- School systems and many educators (though not all) acknowledge, affirm, and reward perfectionistic behavior. You don't get into MIT with a 19 on your ACT. Period.
- Churches and many other religious institutions encourage and affirm unhealthy, Western notions of perfection as virtuous.
- Kids grow up being taught that imperfect behavior "hurts God's feelings" and internalize that they will disappoint God with behavior or performance that is less than perfect.
- We tell young children that they'll end up on Santa's "naughty list" if/when they are flawed in their behavior.

- Parents and other adults pour incredible amounts of resources into helping kids be perfect, for example, private lessons, tutors, and staying up till 3:00 a.m. helping them with assignments.
- Media highlight reels often only show touchdowns, medals, trophies, and huge cash prizes or salaries without showing the years of work, the mismanaged relationships, the lack of balance, and other sacrifices made to a person's relationships and to emotional, mental, and spiritual health that such success often costs.

What Do Adults Need to Know about Perfectionistic Anxiety?

It's About the Anxiety

These are often chronically worried kids whose sympathetic nervous systems are overtaxed and have likely been so for years because of their inability to relax.

It's Not All Driven by Adults

There are many perfectionists out there who drive themselves sick despite their parents and others in their lives encouraging them and attempting to give them permission to "take it easy."

Teens Often Identify Themselves and Judge Their Personal Worth by Their Results

They feel good about themselves when they see results they work so hard to achieve, but even when they separate who they are from what they do (obsessive, perfectionist behavior), they hold on to their anxiety—often very tightly.

Virtuous Work Ethic Can Mask True Anxiety

Some teens hold religious convictions about the importance of maintaining a virtuous work ethic. Often instilled at a young age, this can mask anxiety as a virtue rather than allowing a teen to see real anxiety as anxiety.

How Can Adults Help Perfectionistic Teens?

Acknowledge Your Own Definition of "Success"

This may not seem like the place to start, but if you don't start here, you'll only be rearranging deck chairs on the *Titanic* and dealing with symptoms and not the deeper problem. If you send your kid to therapy to help her stop trying to be perfect but you exhibit and encourage perfectionism, either consciously or unconsciously, your efforts, the counselor's time and effort, and your money may be wasted. Consider how much you advocate for (with words and actions) winning, being the best, and striving for perfection in all things. The questions for reflection at the end of the chapter will help you to process this further.

Ask Your Teen, "What Does It Mean to You to Be Successful?"

* How will you know when you've achieved success?
* What will it look like in one year, two years, three years, ten years, and twenty years?
* What will that feel like?
* Who is the most successful person you know?
* What makes this person successful?
* How does your faith influence how you define success? Or does it?
* What difference would it make if it did?

Normalize Mistakes and Imperfection

When perfectionistic teens make a mistake, this is an opportunity to help them reframe a mistake as "normal" instead of "catastrophic" and "life threatening."

Be Vulnerable

Admit your own mistakes and when appropriate share with teens what those are. This doesn't mean using a teen or a group of teens as your confessor; they don't want or need to know all of your sins and secrets, especially those that would scandalize them or hurt your credibility with them. What you share will depend on how mature the teen is. The older the teen, the more you can share and the more vulnerable you can be. As teens get older, our initiative at being vulnerable rather than compromising our credibility elevates it for them.

Acknowledge and Affirm Attempts to Deal with Their Imperfection

When you see teens make progress at doing things well but shy of perfect, participating even when they can't be the best, sticking with a sport or other activity through the inevitable learning curve, give them sincere, genuine affirmation. That which gets rewarded, gets repeated.

Help Teens Prioritize Tasks

This is difficult for many adults to do, so it might be something you need to practice on your own while helping the teens. Teach them the skill of listing all of their commitments and then ranking them in order of importance. There will be some areas teens feel impossible to rank. In those areas help them prioritize by deciding how much time and energy those items that have equal priority should receive.

Help Teens Recognize When It's Time to Pray to St. GEMO (Which Stands for Good Enough, Move On)

This is a valuable life skill. For perfectionistic teens, who tend to be overachievers, help them to realize that not all tasks and activities are created equal. I'll often tell teens, "Look, you only have 100 percent—total. You can't give 100 percent to everything. You won't get anything done trying to do that." Help them decide the level of time and energy to allocate to each one, and encourage them to do their best within those limits.

Don't Cater to Their Perfectionistic Impulses

Don't go out of your way to accommodate their perfectionism. Set boundaries. Set and enforce end times on work—this is something educators can do as well. Some teens will continue to struggle with perfectionism for all their lives. But they can learn how to manage it, or at least begin managing it, as a teen.

KEY POINTS

- Many young people today are pursuing success without a clear definition of what success really means for them and their lives.
- Many young people believe success is only getting good grades to get into a good college and then make good money.
- This narrow idea of success may be modeled for them by adults, peers, or media personalities, or it may be their own construct.
- Teens need the help of adults to ask themselves what will make them truly happy, not just what they assume will make them happy because of cultural norms. The difference in these two includes factors such as faith, family, community, and service.
- The misunderstanding of Jesus' command to "be perfect, just as your heavenly Father is perfect" (Mt 5:48) has led people of all ages to strive for a perfection more Western and mathematical than spiritual. Jesus' command was closer to, Be perfect in compassion, just as your heavenly Father is.
- Teens need the help of adults to acknowledge, accept, and then change (name, claim, and tame) the things in their lives that they don't like and want to change.
- It is easy for young people to give in to denial because they are still growing in their ability to comprehend and describe their experiences.
- Young people need adults to help them recognize and acknowledge reality. Adults can do this by being authentic and vulnerable.
- Perfectionism is an often-unrecognized form of anxiety.
- Our culture and media frequently focus on achieved success rather than the hard work, suffering, sacrifice, and failures that ultimately made that success possible.
- Perfectionist teens are usually chronically worried youth whose sympathetic nervous system is overtaxed and likely has been for years because of their inability to relax.

- Not all perfectionist teens are driven to those tendencies by the adults in their lives. There are many perfectionists who drive themselves sick despite their parents and others encouraging them to take it easy on themselves.
- Teens identify themselves with their results.
- Perfectionism can be reinforced by religious beliefs held from a young age that mask the anxiety as a virtuous work ethic.

ASK YOURSELF

1. What does it mean for me to be successful?
2. How do I know when I'm successful?
3. Who are the most successful people I know?
4. What makes them successful?
5. How have I come to my definition of success?
6. What did I have to do as a teen to be successful for my parents? Teachers? Coaches? Friends? Others?
7. How do I define success for my child? For my teens?
8. If you're a parent, complete this sentence: "I'll feel successful as a parent if/when my teen _____." (Try to write as much as you can here. The more answers, even seemingly disconnected answers, you generate, the better idea you'll have of what you're communicating, again, consciously or otherwise to your teens about what they have to do to be successful in your eyes.)

FOR INSPIRATION AND PRAYER

So be perfect, just as your heavenly Father is perfect.
—Matthew 5:48

And over all these put on love, that is, the bond of perfection.
—Colossians 3:14

Indeed, though one be perfect among mortals,
   if Wisdom, who comes from you, be lacking,
   that one will count for nothing.
                                        —Wisdom 9:6

There is no one on earth so just as to do good and never
sin.
                                        —Ecclesiastes 7:20

You have been told, O mortal, what is good,
   and what the LORD requires of you:
Only to do justice and to love goodness,
   and to walk humbly with your God.
                                        —Micah 6:8

7. USING THE ROADMAP OF CATHOLIC FAITH

I can't remember the last time I looked at a map on paper. I think it was at a museum for a Civil War battle. Most times, when I need to find a direction to where I'm going, I pull out my phone, open up my maps app, punch in where I want to go, and it shows me the quickest way to get there.

Jeffery, a sixteen-year-old high school sophomore, was once a willingly practicing Catholic. His parents and teachers described him as a faith-filled leader and the kind of kid whom they wished more teens aspired to be like.

But things had changed, as they often do during adolescence. His parents, unbeknownst to him, were in severe conflict. They separated and had "forced amicability" as Jeffery later would describe it. His life would become one of spending one week with Dad at his barely furnished apartment and another week with Mom at the home he'd grown up in. His parents were respectful to one another in front of Jeffery and refused to criticize the other. They also supported one another in parenting and discipline decisions. So when Jeffery developed anxiety and depression, they were both on board to help him and got him into counseling, but not before his anxiety and depression worsened.

Jeffery was having trouble falling asleep at night and described it this way: "I have all these thoughts going on inside my head, and I know you won't believe this, but they're not about my parent's divorce, er, separation. They say it's not a divorce, but I'm not stupid; I know what's coming. I've seen it with my friends several times."

Over the course of a few sessions, I'd ask Jeffery what helped him. He mentioned the classic "hanging out with my friends," which he admitted took up more and more of his time—some of which he once spent with his parents. He also mentioned that sports and exercise helped but that his anxiety was getting so bad he would have panic attacks in the morning before school and again at night before going to bed, which made it even harder to sleep.

At some point I asked Jeffery about his faith, which his parents had mentioned was very important to him. He said, "Yeah, I go to church and stuff."

"What does 'and stuff' mean?" I asked.

"Well, you know, I go to Mass and youth group, and we used to pray as a family, but now most nights Mom drinks wine and watches reality TV. I can tell she's sad and misses Dad. It's weird how parents can miss each other and hate each other at the same time. Does that make sense, Mr. Roy?"

"That makes perfect sense to me, Jeff." I said. "But, and again, I could have misunderstood your dad, but I thought I heard him say that he thought your faith was important to *you*. As I hear you talk about it, it kinda sounds like it's a bit of a drag right now."

"Yeah, I dunno. I just . . . I guess I just lost interest."

"Okay, cool. I just was checking because I know some teens who find comfort and support in their faith practices, and I was just wondering if, at some point in your life, you did the same?" I asked. "I know you're struggling with anxiety, and it's affecting your grades. I'm worried that if we don't nip this anxiety in the bud, it'll turn into depression. Does that make sense?"

Jeff, quite the insightful sophomore, said, "Yeah, I guess worrying all the time and not being able to sleep can make you real depressed."

"Exactly. And you've got a few good tools in your toolbox—friends, exercise, sports. These are all good things. But one thing you no longer have is both parents at home, which at the time didn't seem like a 'tool' to help you cope, but you know how sometimes we don't realize how much something means to us until we lose it? It's kinda like that with our parents. You clearly know it's affecting you, but sometimes we don't realize in what ways or how something helps us to deal with stuff, life and all."

"Wow. I never thought about it like that."

"I guess what I'm curious about is what might you add to your toolbox that, while it won't replace your parents and how important they are, might help in a different way?"

"I dunno," he said.

"I have an idea, and again, I don't know if it'll work or if it's gonna be a fit for you. But there are some things our Catholic faith offers us that can really help when we're struggling. I struggle with anxiety, and man, I don't know what I'd do if it weren't for my faith."

"Okay, well, I guess I'll try anything. I'm open to it."

Over the next few sessions, I gradually introduced one or two tools at a time with the explicit purpose of helping Jeff learn to use his faith as a means of support. We started with the Rosary. I asked him if he could commit to one decade a day, to which he agreed. When he came back the following week he said, "Mr. Roy, it worked okay."

"Well, what does 'okay' mean?"

He said, "Well, it helped a little. But I'm still struggling."

"So is a little better than nothing?" (I ask this because teens often mistakenly assume "help" means "total fix.")

"Well, yeah," he said.

I suggested that between each prayer he take a deep breath and a slow exhale (a variation of square breathing that is very calming). He reported back that it helped even more and that he wanted to add another decade. When I saw Jeff again two weeks later he was up to three decades and fifteen minutes of eucharistic adoration. "I'm hooked, Mr. Roy. It really helps. Like, seriously, I look forward to it."

Jeff would continue to add more of the tools we will discuss later in this chapter. They didn't make his anxiety disappear. But they helped Jeff realize that the tools of our faith are here to help us in every area of our lives, even those areas like mental health that often don't seem at first blush to have anything to do with God. He learned and is still learning, like me, that our God wants to be a part of every area of our lives.

IS FAITH A TOOL?

We are uniquely blessed in our rich Catholic tradition with a multitude of tools to help us when we are faced with challenges in life. I'll name but a few (although it might not seem like just a few), but trust me there are plenty more. Our faith is a gift that keeps on giving. The more we lean into it and the more we grow, the more we discover. At forty-five, I'm still learning about Catholicism, discovering new ways to live out and lean on my faith.

Scientific research has demonstrated time and again that religious belief and practice are helpful in learning to manage anxiety, depression, and other mental health issues.

I GET FAITH, BUT WHY IS RELIGIOUS PRACTICE SO IMPORTANT?

Simply put, religious practice is important because we are human beings and not angels. We have bodies and those real bodies are holy. If we didn't need our bodies to know God, God wouldn't have created them. Unlike some in the past have asserted, our bodies are not evil, nor are they unholy. Much of this was a misinterpretation of St. Paul saying put to death "things of the flesh"(Rom 8:5; see also Rom 8:13). This was an unfortunate translation of the original Greek word *sarx*, which was used for *flesh* in the New Testament. *Sarx* refers to our fallen nature. If Paul were talking about our bodies, he would have used a different Greek word altogether, *soma*, which literally means *body*.

WHAT THEN ABOUT RELIGION?

Unfortunately, for a variety of reasons, many young people see God as a grand royal narcissist who eagerly awaits his subject returning each week, although preferably more often, to pay him homage by genuflecting before, bowing in front of, and revering him. Failure to

do so results in demerits or sins. Getting too many of these means
no heaven for you.

So What Is Religion and Why Do It?

We have religion because *we* need it. God does *not* need us to go to
church and pray. The God of Jesus Christ is a God who doesn't get
hurt when we don't accept his gift of faith. He sure doesn't get mad at
us and use eternal damnation to spite us for it. Isn't it a little absurd
that this is the modus operandi of the vast majority of Catholic Christians? Many Catholics and other Christians tend to relate to God in a
transactional way: "If I do x, God will do y for me." This is a far more
self-centered comprehension of who God is than the Gospel allows
and, frankly, a rather unrefined and underdeveloped conception. We
cannot control or manipulate God's providence; rather, we need to
learn how to understand it, open our hearts and minds to it, and in
the end, welcome it.

We Need Religious Practice

We need to put our finger in the font and put that water on our foreheads and on the chests and shoulders of our T-shirts or designer dress
shirt because we need to know, to remember, that we can only know
through our body that we are washed *clean* by the waters of Baptism.
We are washed clean of sin and, as often as necessary, washed clean
over and over again. We need this and we need to do it as often as
possible until *we* get the deepest truth of all faith—that we are holy.
Our God is an incarnational God who became human so that humans
could become so intimately joined to God that we share in eternal life
even now, through the waters of Baptism. The bodies that too many
of us hate, don't like, or wish were different are in fact imbued with
divine life. They are God's dwelling place.

Deep stuff, huh? I know right?

Our senses often recognize what's important before our wander-
ing minds can pay attention. We need to smell the incense so we can
know, not just with our minds but also with our whole bodies, that
what we're doing is important and holy, so pay attention. We need

to hear bells, smell incense, touch water, taste bread and wine, see candles and Easter fires, smell chrism, and feel it rubbed or poured on our foreheads in order to know with our whole bodies that God is with us. We need rosary beads and Stations of the Cross; we need bibles and prayer books, medals and crucifixes. And we need a community of friends, family, and fellow worshipers to share our stories with, to help us bear our crosses and rejoice in our blessings, and with whom we can utilize our gifts. When our bodies are engaged, not just our intellects, we touch the fullness of God, who after all, became human so we might become God, as St. Athanasius taught in *De incarnatione*, his seminal fourth-century work.

Religion is a tool that helps put us back together with God. But too often young people see us worshiping the tool and not the God. Please read that sentence again. This is like the carpenter who masterfully crafts an incredible mansion sitting down and admiring his hammer and saw! I know carpenters, and they don't do that. They pop open a beer and admire the outcome. Just so, we must witness our personal faith in God (our relationship with God), not simply our membership in and adherence to Church norms and practices. I'm in no way saying that the latter are not crucial to the practice of our faith, but unless teens see the fruits of our relationship with the living God that bring stability and clarity to our lives, they will not come to know the power of true faith. Nor will they consider actively participating in the life of the Church important.

THERE ARE MANY TOOLS IN THE RELIGION TOOLBOX

Sometimes it's easy to overly focus on one tool. There is likely some religious practice that has worked really well for you. Thank God! Keep using it as long as it works. But understand that what works for you may not work for someone else, especially a young person. And what works for young people may not work for you.

For example, over the past twenty or thirty years, we've seen a resurgence of eucharistic adoration. I think this is wonderful. There have been seasons in my life where this devotion has helped me immensely. It gave me something to look at, to focus on, a way to settle my mind and refresh my soul. Adoration begs us to look with our eyes open; it narrows our focus and holds our attention on the person who is most worthy of our attention. Not all young people may like it, but for many, it helps draw them closer to the Lord. It also calms their mind and slows down their thoughts.

WHAT ARE THE VARIOUS TOOLS IN THE RELIGIOUS TOOLBOX THAT CAN HELP YOUNG PEOPLE WHO ARE STRUGGLING?

Sacraments

Eucharist

The Mass helps us participate in several actions that are good for the soul as well as the mind.

1. *A Story Bigger than Ourselves.* It helps young people, even if they're not conscious of it, to know that Jesus suffered, died, and rose again. As bad and as hopeless as teens might feel when their friends talk about them on Snapchat, it helps to know that Jesus also knew betrayal and great sorrow. Recollection of the Paschal Mystery, at the heart of the eucharistic liturgy, shows us, tells us, and feeds us a profound reality. The Eucharist teaches us, deep down in our souls, that we can expect new life to come from death. Young people need to know, just as we do, that even though our struggles may not get immediately better (and may even get worse first), it *will* get better. There is hope to be claimed

in the Paschal Mystery in which we participate every time we go to Mass.

2. *Consistency.* We're living in a world that is in constant flux. The pace of change today is not only dizzying to many adults; it is, often without them realizing it, stressing out young people as well. At a fundamental level we go to the same Mass week after week. Young people and old complain about this, saying, "It's boring, it's the same thing every week." To that I like to respond, "Yes! I know! Isn't that refreshing? I mean by the time Sunday rolls around I'm ready for something familiar." They smile as if to dismiss me, but I can tell they think about it.

3. *Predictability.* There's a predictability within every ritual that soothes us. Knowing what to expect can bring great comfort to busy people who confront vast amounts of information and challenges every day. When we experience life as too unpredictable, we get stressed, anxious, and fearful. Ritual, both big (Mass) and small (a family game night, grace before meals, etc.) stabilizes us in the tumultuous waters of life.

Reconciliation

God does not need us to ask forgiveness. *We need it.* We need to say the thing or things we're ashamed of, embarrassed by, and regret and then watch the priest's head not spontaneously combust. We need to name our sins, own them, and offer them up—give them over to God's healing mercy—through penance or the Sacrament of Reconciliation, so that we can receive the grace to tame our sins. As a counselor, I know firsthand that the value of therapy for many people is simply having a compassionate, nonjudgmental, nonanxious, and listening presence. This is available within the sacrament.

You've no doubt heard young people ask, "Why do I have to go to a priest? Why can't I just tell God my sins and ask forgiveness in my own heart?" I love it when an angry, rage-filled adolescent tells me this, to which I say, "Why did you have to punch a hole in the wall? Why can't you just get mad *in your heart*?" Our bodies are holy and are not just convenient, semi-efficient means of getting our minds from one place to another. We need to say, right out loud, "I have sinned." Saying it makes it more real somehow, and admitting our failings to another human being promises to hold us accountable for mending what our wrongs have caused.

This dynamic is especially good for teens who naturally become narcissistic during adolescence. Saying what they did wrong to another live human being helps to keep them a little humbler than they'd be otherwise. Then, just like the young man in the parable of the prodigal son, they get to experience the loving forgiveness of our heavenly Father.

~~~~~~~~~~~~~~~~

All of the sacraments are sacraments because they draw us into the divine life of the Blessed Trinity. They bind us to the essence of God, which as we explored earlier, is loving relationship. Plunged into the heart of the Trinity through the sacramental life, we find healing, wholeness, and the promise of eternal life.

Baptism, Confirmation, Matrimony, Holy Orders, and Anointing of the Sick give us healing grace whether we are the primary recipient of the sacrament or secondary by being witnesses. I noticed a profound healing in my own life after each of my boys' Baptisms. As adult Catholics who minister with or parent teens, we must learn to witness to our faith by regularly participating in the sacraments and sharing those experiences with our young people.

Prayer

Mental (Internal)

This tool is my personal favorite. I have a naturally contemplative side, and when I steal moments of silence and solitude, I am able to reconnect to myself and to my heart's deepest desires, which are for intimacy with God and sharing God's love with others.

Mental prayer can be powerful for young people today who live amid constant noise, both visual and aural. But it is challenging to get young people, teens especially, to voluntarily quiet themselves and their surroundings in order to receive the rich gifts of silent mental or contemplative prayer.

In my experience, once teens experience contemplative types of prayer, they soon realize its indispensable value to the spiritual life. As one teen said to me, "I don't how I lived without it." Introducing contemplative prayer to young people usually requires great courage and confidence. Often this means asking teens to put away (lock up even) their phones/devices and asking them to trust that God's "still, small voice" is enough for them. It won't work for every kid, but it does for many.

As I mentioned earlier, I believe that eucharistic adoration is doing this for young people. Many ministers begin with music and singing and even visual effects and slowly reduce the stimulation and lead the group to silence. This is often a very powerful prayer experience. You'd want to use good pastoral judgment based on the age, maturity, and experience level of your group as how best to achieve this.

Verbal

When given the opportunity, many young people will pray aloud. To lift their voices to God in prayer, they will often pray first for the needs of others before, if ever, getting to themselves. This is particularly common with kids who are marginalized and neglected. I'll often recommend that teens pray aloud, even when they are alone. When we hear our voice reaching out to God, it sends a signal to our brain that says, "Hey, I'm really doing something here." It also helps teens to hear what's on their own hearts. With everything that's competing for their attention and that often gets jumbled up in their brains, praying aloud helps them to slow down their minds; hear their thoughts, dreams, hopes, and desires; and then begin to make sense of them.

Communal

There's just something about praying in a group of other people that lets us know, on a deep level, that we're not alone. This is one of the great pains and fears of today's young people: they feel alone.

Communal prayer helps this, whether it's petitionary prayer, liturgical prayer, eucharistic adoration and other devotions, or quiet time reflecting together. Young people have a unique opportunity to learn that church is not a private affair and that others are often struggling with the same issues they are. Special attention should be given to age and maturity level in this type of prayer. Young people should be prepared by way of knowing what to expect, to be respectful of others, and what appropriate and inappropriate behavior would look like. Often we expect kids to know things we wouldn't have known at their age.

Catholic Devotions

The Rosary and Divine Mercy Chaplet

The Rosary and Divine Mercy Chaplet are wonderful for teens who need something to do with their hands. When I am frazzled or too much in my head, nothing centers me like rolling my fingers over those beads and mouthing the prayers/mantras over and over while contemplating the mysteries of Jesus' life. For teens who are kinesthetically oriented or have trouble focusing attention, prayer beads can be a marvelous way for them to calm themselves and open their minds and hearts to God.

Novenas

From the Latin word *nine*, most novenas are a series of prayers, often for a special intention, that span the length of nine days. Beautiful psychology! Taking on a commitment to pray from one's heart for an intention for an undetermined length of time can be overwhelming for many young people, and they'll often not start. When they know there's an ending time and you give them the words to pray, it becomes very doable.

Sacred Scripture

What a treasure trove of hope, peace, and inspiration is sacred scripture! Often people, young and old, avoid the scriptures because the language, in certain parts, is dense. For beginners, suggesting specific verses from the New Testament for different struggles they're having can be very helpful. For all age and maturity levels, I'd especially recommend *Follow*, a resource by Katie Prejean McGrady. This is a magnificent handbook of accessible and practical how-tos of living out one's faith as a young person. The chapters on prayer and scripture references are unparalleled in my opinion.

Pilgrimages

We can access just about anything online today either through recorded means or a live stream. Yet there's something about being there, and for pilgrimages, often *getting* there, that adds a huge spiritual component one cannot get through a screen. The bonding and the struggles of the shared journey—as is often the case on a pilgrimage—are irreplaceable. In the words of my friend Maria, who founded Magnificat Travel, a ministry of bringing people old and young alike on pilgrimages, "Reminder, this is a pilgrimage, not a tour or a vacation!" Learning how to deal with adversities and struggles in group settings on a journey is a great metaphor for life. Making this element explicitly clear to young people before, during, and after helps them to deepen that aspect of the experience.

There's also something to be said about a change of scenery and environment. Service learning experiences, mission trips, or pilgrimages to holy places help us to naturally reflect on our journey. Just as we would on any trip think about the place we've left behind, where we are now, and our final destination, the same happens internally for the spiritual and emotional journeys we have undertaken.

Retreats

As someone who loves retreats and has taken more young people on retreat over the years than I can remember, I can testify firsthand how powerful these experiences of "retreating" from everyday life can be. Good, well-planned, well-staffed, well-executed retreats can be life changing. When parents ask me, I have rarely counseled them not to send their child on a retreat.

If, however, a teen is struggling with something specific, especially anxiety or depression; is self-harming; or is having suicidal thoughts, all pertinent adults should consult together and at an appropriate time with the teen. This way a sound decision as to whether the teen's attending that particular retreat at that particular time is the right thing for the teen as well as for the other retreatants.

Retreats can be emotional, often *very* emotional, and when appropriate, can be very cathartic and healing. When the timing is off, it can be a train wreck. The retreat director will be able to help you determine if a kid is ready for that type of experience. If parents come to you and ask you that question, you might want to refer them back to a counselor or you can ask the parents or teen to sign a release for you to talk with the counselor, so you can all together, including the teen, make the best decision.

Visiting Burial Places

Another huge yet often unappreciated and underutilized tool of our faith is the practice of visiting and praying for the dead at cemeteries and mausoleums. There's something about going to the burial place of a loved one or holding the remains of a loved one that can pull the grief out of us and help us with healing as does nothing else. I've lost track of how often I encourage parents and young people to go to the grave of a loved one. If it's soon after their death or if the young people might not be able to control their emotions, going with someone is a good idea. If however, they can and have a desire to go by themselves, a parent or friend could drop them off and wait, or if they're old enough and able, they can drive themselves. Part of the catharsis is tears. Jesus modeled this for us at Lazarus's tomb: "And Jesus wept" (Jn 11:35). Some wounds in our lives can only be wept over, and those tears are as holy as any water in any font in any church in the world.

Our faith tells us that the faithful who have died remain with us in a very real way. We remain united with them in the Communion of Saints, and so to honor, connect with, and pray to, for, and with them at the place of burial is a laudable practice.

Faith and religious practice are not therapy, and I'm not suggesting that anyone with serious mental health and emotional issues can simply "pray it away." I am suggesting, however, that regardless of how serious an issue is or how difficult a challenge a young person is facing, faith and religious practice can help alongside counseling, medication, and other tools.

I see all too often religious faith being disregarded in place of things that "work." I have seen firsthand, in my own life and in the lives of teens in my psychotherapy practice, the indispensable role faith plays in the healing process and as a set of coping tools. As Catholic adults caring for youth, we serve them best by witnessing the faith and gently helping them discover which of our religious practices can help them in their journey toward better mental, emotional, and spiritual health.

KEY POINTS

- Research has shown that religious practice and having a belief system are therapeutic in overcoming anxiety, depression, and other mental health issues.
- We need to participate in religious rituals and practices as human beings to connect our mortal experience with the immortal reality of the divine.
- Religion is a tool that can put us back together with God.
- The various tools in the "Catholic toolbox"—ranging from various forms of prayer, scripture, song, and above all, the sacraments—connect young people with God and others and are invaluable resources in coping with stress, anxiety, and depression.

ASK YOURSELF

1. Write about some ways that your own religious belief and practice has helped you in your struggles with stress and anxiety.
2. What did faith and religious practice mean to me as a young person? What role did they fill in my life then?
3. How has my outlook on faith and religious practices changed as I've grown older?
4. Have I ever noticed a correlation in my own life between increased stress and anxiety and a lack of prayer or other religious and spiritual activity?

FOR INSPIRATION AND PRAYER

For as in one body we have many parts, and all the parts do not have the same function, so we, though many, are one body in Christ and individually parts of one another.
—Romans 12:4–5

And I tell you, ask and you will receive; seek and you will find; knock and the door will be opened to you. For everyone who asks, receives; and the one who seeks, finds; and to the one who knocks, the door will be opened.
—Luke 11:9–10

They devoted themselves to the teaching of the apostles and to the communal life, to the breaking of the bread and to the prayers.
—Acts 2:42

8. LEARNING THE ART OF LISTENING

Braylin, a very bright, fourteen-year-old ninth grader, like so many girls her age, was bullied by a group of mean girls at her middle school. What her parents described as this once bright, confident, assertive, beautiful, and joyful girl had lost not only her confidence but also her joy.

Middle school is a challenging time for most young people. The combination of physical, emotional, social, and spiritual growth during those years is often confusing at best and disorienting at worst. It's normal to see some changes in young people during this time, but these were so drastic and sudden it merited more attention. In addition, her grades were beginning to drop.

When I first sat with Braylin, she was scared. I mean, she was four feet tall and weighed maybe a hundred pounds, and I'm a six-foot-one bald guy who weighs twice what she does. I'm not Vin Diesel by any stretch, but for younger kids, my size and unguarded extroverted personality can be intimidating.

When I asked her to tell me about herself, she said, "I dunno. There's not much that's worth talking about."

"What do you mean?" I asked.

"Well, I just don't have much about me that's interesting," she said, still sitting on the edge of my sofa looking down at her feet.

"Really? You're in ninth grade!" I said somewhat loudly, trying to get her to look at me. "I've never met a ninth grader who wasn't interesting. What do you like to do for fun?"

Older teens with good social relationships normally answer this question with, "Hang out with my friends." I did know she liked dancing.

"I dunno. I haven't had fun in a while," she said sadly.

"Mmm. I hear ya. So for you, right now, is it kinda like, 'I just can't seem to have fun anymore'?" I asked.

"Yeah. And I want to, and I even try. My parents tell me I'm not trying, but I am Mr. Peda— How do you pronounce your last name again?" she asked with a scared look on her face that it just might be pronounced like the word "pedophile" but didn't want to say that at risk of offending me. I'd seen this before.

"It's not 'pedophile' if that's what you're wondering!" I laughed and smiled big, which caused her to show me that beautiful smile her parents were beginning to forget.

"It's peh-tuh-feece. It's a really hard name to pronounce. I know. Don't worry if you mess it up. You can just call me P or Mr. P if that's okay." Again, she laughed a bit. I knew this was as much fun as she'd allow herself to have during our session or else she'd be upset with me for fixing her too quickly. She'd also be mad at herself, because if a stranger can make her feel better that fast, why couldn't she do it?

"What's it like for you when Mom and Dad tell you, 'Braylin, just try to be happy'?"

"It's like, 'Seriously? Do you think I like feeling like this? I mean I'm depressed for God's sake; it's not like I want to be sad all the time.'"

"I hear ya. So is it kinda like, 'Come on guys, really? Do you think I woke up one morning and said to myself, "You know what would be great? Being depressed and not having any fun. That would be *awesome*! I'm gonna get right to work and make that happen."'"

"Exactly! Finally, someone understands!" she said loudly and leaned back on the couch as if a huge weight was lifted off her shoulders.

WHY IS LISTENING SO HARD?

Many factors, including the following, make listening difficult:

- our desire or need to fix
- our need to be right

- our false sense of urgency
- our fears of having not said the right thing driving us to constantly think about what we should say
- misinterpreting teens who say, "They didn't know what to say; so they weren't actually helpful." In doing this, teens are suggesting that what would help them is for us to "say the right thing." It can create pressure for the listening adult. As one adult told me, "I knew listening wasn't enough. I knew I should have said something." In the vast majority of cases, good listening and reflecting back what we are hearing to teens, using the skills in this chapter, is what the teen really wants from us as opposed to advice, which is often not helpful.
- our own need to be heard and understood
- being verbal processors
- not understanding what the teen is trying to communicate
- teens saying the same thing every time and not doing anything about it—that is, feeling powerless
- feeling as if you're not doing anything meaningful or important

WHAT IS RESISTANCE?

Whenever we find ourselves trying to get teens to do something, believe something, choose something, or value something and they choose not to do it, there is resistance. Every day I study human resistance, especially among adolescents. When teenagers come into my office and I see the daggers they throw at me from their eyes or notice them slump down into the sofa in my office, I know they have no interest in being there and are only there because someone made them come. It is at this point that most of us adults who catch these nonverbal cues get defensive—in other words, we either take it personally and make the resistance about us or we ignore it and move right ahead with our agenda. Both approaches will only increase the resistance.

What Does Resistance Look Like?

The first task is recognizing the signs of adolescent resistance. We see it in

- apathy, or an "I don't care" attitude;
- tone of voice, for example, a hostile tone or using curt sentences;
- word choices and use of phrases such as "I don't want to be here," "I'm being forced to be here," and "Yeah, but . . ." as a response to something you've suggested;
- posture, as resistance can be indicated by either an excessively withdrawn posture or an aggressive posture;
- facial expressions such as smirks, eye-rolling, and raised eyebrows; and
- refusal to accept a logical argument.

While all of these are signs of resistance, it would be wrong to interpret them as saying, "I'm never going to listen to you." It is better to read these signs as saying, "I'm not ready—yet—to communicate with you." The way we approach a teen who is exhibiting these signs will affect how we deal with the resistance.

Ineffective Ways of Dealing with Resistance

Increase Volume

Many believe that when others don't respond to our verbal messages, be they suggestions, requests, or commands, if we say them louder or more frequently we will achieve the desired result. This indicates a fundamental lack of understanding of people and the power of resistance. It also assumes that people make changes because of logic. Not so.

Increase Logic

You may make minor changes in your life based on logical reasoning, but most people cannot successfully make major life changes without an emotionally charged reason to do so. Often this reason is discovered within the context of a relationship marked by high levels of trust, caring, and understanding. Increasing the volume of our voice and the frequency of what we want to say only increases resistance and makes it that much harder to communicate our message.

~~~~~~~~~~~~~~~~~

If you've ever heard yourself saying, "How many times do I have to tell you?" or raising your voice with a teen (which is usually because we don't feel heard), that's a cue you're running into resistance. Depending on the nature of your relationship with the teen, if you are a parent or teacher, you may be encountering this resistance while trying to handle an issue that merits a consequence. I will discuss consequences in greater detail in a later chapter.

Four Types of Resistance

Intellectual

Examples of intellectual resistance include expressing a different point of view, disagreeing with someone's logic or reasoning, and feigning ignorance. Addressing this type of resistance is a strength of our Catholic Church. We have a rich tradition of providing philosophical, theological, and biblical support for the tenets of our faith. Today, however, intellectual resistance in many teens is less about the inherent validity of matters of faith and much more about how those assertions of faith can be reconciled with the empirical discoveries being made in the hard sciences.

This can be a challenging area for adults who care about teens. Some adults who don't know how to address those important questions enjoy researching to find the answers and the best ways to explain them to teens. But I've heard many adults tell me over the years, "Roy, I want to help them, but I don't have the answers to their questions, and I don't have time or the inclination to look them up." You definitely don't have to be a scientist or a theologian to accompany teens. I've worked with many teens who were intellectually gifted and were able to put me through my paces. Sometimes I would say,

"Hey, I want to answer your questions but I can't. Would you consider talking to someone else who is better equipped to answer your
questions?" This will usually earn you the teen's respect. Teens know
when we don't know the answers, and if we try to act as if we do, we
lose their respect. It's always okay to say "I don't know," "I'll look it
up," or "I'll ask" or even recommend they talk with someone else.

Emotional

Often teens' seemingly intellectual questions about faith mask a deeper, more emotional question. Trying to answer an emotional question
with an intellectual answer often causes emotional resistance. This
type of resistance usually results from an experience of disappointment coming from being wounded or let down. It is very common,
especially with young people when they cannot place blame on someone or something else. Common examples of emotional resistance
in young people is the experience of someone close to them dying, a
natural disaster, or a major disruption in family life such as divorce.
When all else fails, the blame will either consciously or unconsciously
be ascribed to God.

Saying "I'm agnostic," "I'm an atheist," or "Christians are just a
bunch of hypocrites" are symptoms of emotional resistance that are
often mistaken for intellectual resistance. These sound better than
saying, "I'm having some feelings about God and the Church I don't
understand," or "I'm angry that God . . ." or "My parents are divorced
but I still love them both, and because I cannot give myself permission
to be mad at them, I'll blame God for allowing them to get a divorce."
Such awareness is rarely found in adolescents. Even those few who
do possess such high levels of emotional awareness probably won't
share it in a classroom, youth group meeting, or Confirmation class.

You can make the most compelling case for apostolic succession,
but if a young person says he hates the pope because he represents a
God whom he believes took his father, you're wasting your time. The
best way to address emotional resistance is to roll with it. Fighting it,
arguing against it, or trying to persuade someone out of it will only
increase its intensity and make your ministry (and possibly your life)
more difficult.

Young people who act resistant need acceptance and permission to be where they are and feel what they feel. Most importantly, they need to have a safe place to express themselves freely. If you become that safe place, you have the privilege of showing them a more accurate and loving picture of the God they resist. (All of the above applies not only to young people but to young and older adults as well.)

Spiritual

Sin is a choice to step out of relationship with Christ. The more seriously and repeatedly we move away from him, the more resistant we become to reentering and mending that relationship. In other words, there is a cumulative effect in unrepented sin that drives us away from Christ.

Physical

Many people experience, learn, and process kinesthetically—touching, moving, creating, and yes, even destroying. This is often true of males in particular. I've seen some highly resistant young people open up while mixing cement in Mexico, while riding horses, or after they rocketed to the clouds as a result of jumping onto a giant air pillow in a mountain lake.

OWNING OUR NEED TO BE RIGHT

I once heard it said, "It's not good enough to be right. We must seek to be effective." You're reading this book because you want to be effective. Effectively influencing teens starts with meeting them where they are, not inviting them to you. Unless the situation is an emergency, give yourself permission to slow down or postpone the discussion until you have the time and can muster the energy to empathize. If you don't, you won't be influential, and you will likely increase the resistance in the relationship.

When we get into repeating the same thing over and over, what young people (and any other age group really) hear is, "It's all about me and my agenda. Listen carefully to me, because I'm right and I've got something important to say." That's not what we intend to communicate, but because that's what young people hear, it is precisely what we are communicating. There is a wise adage that reminds us of this dynamic: "I don't know what I said until you tell me what you heard."

The fact is that too many adults will not surrender their agendas, as virtuous and noble as they may be, in order to create the best opportunity to positively influence a young person. Many adults get caught up in a need to be right instead of focusing on what they must do to reach teenagers. Being right is not the same thing as accuracy. Accuracy is an objective reality. Either the widget is or isn't green. If it is green, it is immaterial whether or not I acknowledge that it is green. The widget is green—nothing I say will change that reality.

Being right, on the other hand, is a need of the ego. The green widget doesn't need you to advocate for its greenness; it will be green regardless. When you need me to agree with you or when you get upset that I don't agree with you, that's a clear indicator that you are more concerned with being right than with being effective. Your need for young people to see a situation the way you do comes from your ego's need to be right.

EARNING THE RIGHT TO BE HEARD

The days of young people doing what adults tell them to just because an adult told them to are long gone. "Father says," "Sister says," "The teacher says," and even "Mom or Dad says" don't produce the effect they did when I was a kid in the 1970s and 1980s. Your title or role in the life of young people matters significantly less than your having earned the right to be heard.

This is another reason listening is so important. *It earns you the right to be heard*, especially when followed by good questions. And when we have earned the right to be heard, then, and *only* then, can we influence young people.

THE ISLAND OF "IT SHOULDN'T BE THAT WAY"

Times have changed, and trying to influence young people in the drastically more complex culture than the one we grew up in leaves many adults distressed and saying, "But it shouldn't be that way!" Maybe, maybe not, but things are this way. We could fill up countless pages with things, situations, and changes taking place in the world that shouldn't be but are. So while we're bemoaning what shouldn't be, many of the things that do bring real harm to our youth continue to worsen as we adults find it more and more difficult to reach them in effective ways.

When you find yourself saying, "It shouldn't be that way," what you're doing, often unconsciously, is ascribing an unfathomable amount of complexity to a situation, an issue, or a problem that you believe must be a result of some cosmic force beyond your control. This gives you an excuse to not change; to not invest time, energy, and effort in understanding the nature of the problem; and to not act. In short, "it shouldn't be that way" often becomes a cop-out.

When you find yourself thinking or saying, "It shouldn't be this way," acknowledge your frustration: "I'm up against a problem I perceive to be so large and complex that I can't understand it and I feel utterly helpless to influence the situation." Recognizing and naming what's going on inside of us when we encounter adolescent resistance (or any other seemingly insurmountable problem) is the first step to addressing it.

Once we acknowledge our own fears, we can step up and step in: "Right now I don't have enough information and skills to address this problem." Now you've opened a pathway to the solution. With more information, you will have increased understanding. There are many ways to get the information you need, none of them better than asking the teens themselves. A phrase I use in just about every session is, "I want to understand what you're going through. Help me understand." When you express this with sincerity and authenticity, teens will often reward you with a treasure trove of new information. Additionally, you can read blogs like mine at todaysteenager.com or

Life Teen's, at lifeteen.com, which is a rich source of current information about teens. One other resource would be the Center for Parent/ Youth Understanding at cpyu.org. All three of these resources have information, tools, and skills for any adult who cares about teens. And with new information, tools, and skills, you will grow in your confidence to address the issue.

HOW CAN I OVERCOME RESISTANCE?

Recognizing resistance is the first hurdle. You can't overcome an enemy you don't see. The next challenge is dealing with the resistance. Here are some tips for overcoming the resistance that occurs when we are trying to help teens.

Listen for the Question behind the Question

If someone asks a question about abortion, such as "How can the Church say that abortion is a mortal sin? I mean it's a woman's body; it's her right to choose," before jumping into a defensive rant, ask, "I'd love to address your question. [Don't say *answer* because you may decide not to answer the question.] Would it be okay with you though, if first you shared with me [or with the group, if you are in that setting] your own feelings and opinions about the Church's teaching on abortion?" They're going to listen to you only after they feel heard and understood. What they really might be asking is, "Am I [or my friend or my mom] going to hell because I [or she] had an abortion?"

Practice the Skill of Active Listening

Pay close attention to what is being said. Repeat back to teens what you are hearing, and ask if they think you understand them.

Acknowledge and Validate Feelings and Opinions

Everyone is entitled to his or her own feelings and opinions. Yet if you make one eye roll, one sneer, or one disparaging sideways glance to another person in the room, you're toast. The teen will feel disrespected, and this will only reinforce whatever feelings or opinions the teen currently has about adults, God, the Church, and Christianity.

WHAT IS HELPFUL
ABOUT LISTENING?

* When others are able to understand our story or experience, it helps us to better understand theirs.
* When we feel heard, we feel less alone.
* When someone gives us his or her undivided attention, we feel important and cared about.

WHAT ARE THE SKILLS
OF LISTENING?

People often tell me, "Roy, I'm just not a good listener." While some things come naturally to some people and are learned unintentionally, the fact remains that most people have to learn skills if they want to do something well. Riding a bike requires a skill set that is often learned through practice and repetition. Listening is no different. Here are some of the skills one can learn to become a good listener.

Eye Contact

This can be tricky. Looking others in the eyes can make them feel vulnerable. It may even make *you* feel vulnerable. Getting young people to be vulnerable by our words and our actions, at times, is a good thing. But too much too soon or at the wrong time can leave them feeling overexposed. When teens feel overexposed, they may feel embarrassed, and no one likes embarrassment, especially self-conscious young people. You risk losing contact, connection, or the relationship with teens if you overexpose them. Yet many young people today spend their days looking into their cell phones, tablets, computers, and the like, so the amount of real eye contact they experience is minimal. When we adults engage with teenagers in this way, it has an impact on them, even if only unconsciously. Go carefully here.

There is a saying "The eyes are the window to the soul." By making and keeping good eye contact, we communicate genuine interest. And in a very powerful way, we communicate to teens that they are important.

Pay Attention

The word "pay" is important here because *attention* is perhaps our most precious commodity. We only have so much of it to go around, so when we give it, we are making a real investment or paying a significant price. When we invest the gift of our attention to young people, the return we get is an opportunity to reach them in a unique way.

Paying attention is hard. But it's important because when we drift away from being present to young people, not only do they notice but also we're missing potentially critical information that may not be coming through in their words. A teen might say "I love my dad" with a big smile on her face and other facial expressions that let you know she really means it. Then again, she might say "I love my dad" in an unconvincing tone, facial expression somewhat flat and looking away. If you're not paying attention, you're missing crucial information from her. She's saying the words, but she doesn't mean them. It's incongruent. Why she is saying that she loves her dad may be worth exploring. You might say something like this: "Really? I mean, we don't need to talk about it now, but I dunno, there's something about the way you said that that left me wondering if you meant it. I don't doubt that you love your dad, but I'm just wondering if there's more you want to say about him or about loving your dad." If it's not the right time, the teen will say "nah," or if it is she might tell you more. But she'll only tell you more if she sees that you're paying attention.

I sometimes have kids, teens, and young adults *intentionally* say things with nonverbals that are incongruent just to see if I am paying attention. They are doing a psychological version of "toe dipping" to test the waters and make sure it's safe to get in or, in this case, let out what they're considering saying. Young people, especially teens, are constantly "toe dipping" to assess whether or not we're safe and paying attention.

It's really easy to be inattentive when we've gotten to know someone really well. You may pick up on cues that interpret as, "I've heard this before; I can relax. I know what's coming." The truth is, you may or may not know what's coming. Furthermore, that's a very pragmatic view of the value of listening. Sometimes, young people just need us to hear them say the same things over and over again because their friends are tired of it. We'll discuss this more later in this chapter, but just "hearing them out" is incredibly valuable to young people. But to do that we need to be paying attention.

Listen for What's Being Said and What's Not

Sometimes young people will tell you everything you need to know, yet just as often they will leave out important information. For instance, if a teen spends the whole session with me talking about her mom, I'm also hearing that she's choosing to say nothing about her dad. Teens may say a lot about their family but nothing about their friends. That may not mean anything. But it may. It might not be something you bring up in the moment, but you could create a mental note to revisit that one day. You might say something like, "You know we never seem to talk about your dad. Tell me about him, what's he like."

QUESTIONS ARE MORE IMPORTANT THAN ANSWERS

For too many years in school I collected a ton of answers in the way of information. For years, those answers lined my bookshelves as binders of written notes that I'd collected from almost thirty-three years in school. When I began counseling I noticed that my answers weren't helping my young clients. I could see what the problem was and tell them exactly how to fix it, but they resisted. This was frustrating! *Why won't you listen to me?* I thought. Early on I realized that my clients were thinking the exact same thing. I struggled with this because I didn't know how I could listen when they were not talking. I discovered that young people didn't want my answers; they wanted me to ask powerful questions and then listen intently, as if my life depended on it, to *their* answers.

I went on a search to collect such questions. I began writing them down and cataloging them so that in any situation with a teen I had not just one question but a series of questions from different angles that helped me start and maintain dialogue with a teen who would otherwise not offer much during our conversation. I've included most of them in this book, but I'd encourage you to begin a collection of your own. You may choose to use some you've found here and from other places. Some great questions to ask other adults who work with teens are, "How would you go about asking a teen about this? How would you go about discussing this issue with this teen? What would you say?" If what they say resonates with you, put it in your own words and write it down.

Be Aware of Your Assumptions

As frequently as possible, begin interactions with an open mind. This is not easy, but it's difficult to see the reality of the young person in front of us when our vision is being blurred by our preconceptions and assumptions. Adolescence is a time of rapid change on every level. When I was teaching in the classroom, I had a note on my desk that read, "These are not the same kids that were here yesterday; get to know these kids."

Smile

The majority of teens today are wary of adults. They don't necessarily assume that we're mean or out to get them; they just don't tend to trust us. A genuine smile tells them we're not the enemy. It also tells them they are someone worth smiling at.

Ask Open-Ended Questions and Listen

Even if their answers are brief or they act a little weird about this, it is usually because they are nervous. But teenagers like the attention and appreciate your effort to let them know you care about what they think. When we make a habit of asking them questions and then patiently listening to them while they answer, teens feel seen. They experience this as us focusing on them in a positive way, and it contributes to their positive self-esteem. It's another opportunity to build trust and a pathway for open communication.

REFLECT BACK WHAT YOU HEAR: ECHO CHAMBER

A teen once told me that he didn't like his school counselor: "I couldn't tell if he was listening. I mean it seemed like he was, but I never knew if he understood me or not. Humph, now that I think about it, I don't know if he wanted to understand me or not." Even skilled, seasoned counselors can neglect this simple skill. let young people know what you're hearing them say and ask them if what you're hearing is actually what they're trying to say.

A teen might approach you saying, "I hate this school. I wanna leave and never come back. If I could just go back to my old school, I would be so happy!"

A possible echo might be, "So for you, right now, is it kinda like 'Man I just hate this school. Life started really sucking when I got here. I just wish I could go back to my other school where at least there were some familiar people and I had some friends'?"

This type of echoing back gives young people power to say yes or no, indicating whether or not our understanding matched what they were trying to say. In any adult–teen relationship, there is always a power differential, regardless of how brazen the young person is, because they and we know that in general adults have the power. Because of this, young people also want us to be right, so if you're stating it as a fact, they may question themselves saying, "I didn't think I really hated it here that bad, but maybe I do." But if you put it forth tentatively, by saying the words "Is it kind of like . . ." the young person gets the chance to respond in a few different ways, including "Yeah, exactly." or "Hmm, not really." Paying attention to their nonverbals here is key because they'll tell you if you're really understanding it all or not.

If a kid says, "Yeah, I guess that's it . . ." that means it's *not* it. You should say, "Okay, it doesn't sound like I understand fully what you're trying to say/going through. I wonder what part I'm missing." Whereas if they say, "Exactly," that means you got it. Sometimes, older teens will say "yeah . . ." but then continue speaking because you put it forth tentatively, they know you respect them and their experience, and they will continue to say more to help you understand what they're saying.

As is always the case for young people regardless of their age—be they preteens or college-age young adults—until their prefrontal cortex is fully grown (which is around the age of twenty-five), they are always trying to find the right language for their experience. And if you remember back in chapter 2, one of the best ways we help young people is by helping them find the language to match their experience. When we can name what we're going through, regardless of how tough it is, we have a sense of control over it and feel less at the whim of our (strong) emotions.

Listening to young people is a powerful and crucial skill that not only lets them know you understand but also validates their inherent dignity as a child of God. Listening well by paying attention, asking clarifying questions, and reflecting back what you hear tells that young person—often in ways they cannot yet describe—that you care and that they are important. This is how Jesus helped people feel.

KEY POINTS

- Truly listening to a young person is a powerful skill and service that can have a profound, positive impact on that young person.
- Listening is, however, extremely difficult. Our need to fix and be right and our fear of not knowing what to say or not say and of misunderstanding a young person often keep adults from attentively listening to young people.
- Whenever we find ourselves trying to get teens to do something, believe something, choose something, or value something, and they choose not to do it, there is resistance.
- Resistance in a teen is often manifested in apathy, tone of voice, posture, word choice, facial expressions, or refusal to hear a logical argument. These signs should be interpreted by adults as "I'm not ready to communicate yet" instead of "I will never communicate with you."
- There are four forms of resistance: intellectual, emotional, spiritual, and physical.
- Effectively influencing teens starts with meeting them where they are, not inviting them to be where we are.
- Many adults get caught up in a need to be right instead of focusing on what they must do to reach teenagers.
- An adult who listens to a young person earns the right to be heard. Only when we have earned the right to be heard can we influence young people.
- When others are able to understand our story or experience, it helps us do the same.
- When we feel heard, we feel less alone.
- When someone gives us his or her undivided attention, we feel important and cared about.
- When we invest the gift of our attention to young people, the return we get is an opportunity to reach them in a unique way.
- The majority of teens today are wary of adults.
- Listening well by paying attention, asking clarifying questions, and echoing back what you hear tells young people, often in ways they may not be able to describe, that you care and that they are important.

ASK YOURSELF

1. Three people who listened well to me when I was a young person are _____.
2. How did the attentive listening of these people help me feel important and heard?
3. Three people to whom I did not attentively listen in the last day are _____.
4. What kept me from truly listening?
5. Who is the best listener in my adult life? What qualities make that person a good listener?
6. Choose one of the qualities from the last question, and write a one-sentence plan for integrating those qualities in your interactions with the people in your life who need to be heard.

FOR INSPIRATION AND PRAYER

The LORD will pass by. There was a strong and violent wind rending the mountains and crushing rocks before the LORD—but the LORD was not in the wind; after the wind, earthquake—but the LORD was not in the earthquake; after the earthquake, fire—but the LORD was not in the fire; after the fire, a light silent sound. When he heard this, Elijah hid his face in his cloak and went out and stood at the entrance of the cave.

—1 Kings 19:11b–13a

While he was at table in his house, many tax collectors and sinners came and sat with Jesus and his disciples. The Pharisees saw this and said to his disciples, "Why does your teacher eat with tax collectors and sinners?" [Jesus] heard this and said, "Those who are well do not need a physician, but the sick do. Go and learn the meaning of the words, 'I desire mercy, not sacrifice.' I did not come to call the righteous but sinners."

—Matthew 9:10–13

Fools take no delight in understanding,
but only in displaying what they think.
—Proverbs 18:2

9. FINDING HELP
FOR·THE HELPER

Working in isolation with young people is dangerous for you and for them—perhaps not physically dangerous, but even that is possible. When our work with them is in the open, in the light, both they and we are above board morally, legally, and emotionally.

Working with teens—and certainly parenting them—is emotionally challenging. You will not survive as a parent or other caring adult, whether you are a professional or a volunteer, if you try to go it alone. You need others for emotional support, feedback, creative ideas, and fresh perspective and to remind you often that you are not crazy—except for the fact that you're working with young people.

REMEMBERING OUR ROLE

I always felt a call to help young people who were hurting. As you know from my story, I have a deep well of empathy from which that call springs forth. Yet over the years in my role as a teacher and minister, I had to be reminded that I was not a trained, licensed therapist. That was tough for me. It was so tough that after one of those reminders, I enrolled in graduate school to earn a degree in counseling. Today, as painful as they were, I am grateful for those reminders. I am grateful because I was, in those instances, right and wrong. Wrong in that I was in over my head in attempting to deal with issues in which I was not trained. Thankfully, no young people were hurt because I didn't *think* the teen was suicidal or needed counseling. I was right in that many young people will open up to ministers. And those ministers, like me, need to be equipped with skills ranging from listening all the way to making a referral to a mental health professional.

Parents, educators, and ministers need additional tools from the social sciences that will help augment the work you do in your particular setting. The key word here is *augment*, "add to."

We are all "counselors" in as much as counsel is a gift of the Holy Spirit. That being said, there comes a point with some young people when they need more help than you can give. Some young people struggle with things that need specialized help from a trained, licensed, experienced professional. If you're like me, that last sentence might upset you a bit. You may recognize within you the gift of counsel, the natural ability to build rapport with young people and get them to open up to you. You might feel compelled to remind me at this point that I said earlier in the book that 90 percent of what I do is listen, and you feel you are a natural listener. If this is you, let me say this: I've been there, and I've been where I am now. I can no longer do what you do for young people, and honestly you cannot, without the training, supervision, and years of practice, do what I do for young people. In the words of Mother Teresa, "I cannot do what you can do. You cannot do what I can do. But together, we can do something beautiful for God."

For too long, religion and the social sciences have operated in silos with a mutual distrust of the other. Thankfully, today those silos are collapsing in the name of collaboration. But we still have a long way to go. One thing is for certain: the young people in our care benefit most when we work together in a spirit of collaboration.

SO, HOW DO I KNOW
WHEN I'M IN OVER MY HEAD?

It is important, not only for the young people in your care but also for your own self-care, that you are able to recognize when a young person needs more help than you can offer.

Honestly, this will be trial and error. You'll have to find your way within this depending on your own particular skill set and the policies of the school, parish, diocese, or other organization where you interact regularly with teens. As a parent, your own intuition and comfort level along with the advice of others in your support network will be key factors in determining when it's time to get help for those who know more than you about a particular area of concern. There are a few issues that are "no brainers" when you must make a referral to a professional. We'll discuss later in the chapter what those are and the best practices for referring.

Before listing specific situations and issues, let me offer a few guiding principles.

Do No Harm

This is the single most important ethic or guideline for any helper, whether a minister, teacher, therapist, or doctor. This simply means that regardless of my desire to help and regardless of my skill set, training, and expertise, I must always weigh the potential benefit of whatever I'm considering against the potential for that action to cause harm. Ask yourself the following:

- Whom could I reach out to/consult with to help guide me here?
- What's the risk of having this conversation? Saying this? Not saying this?
- What might happen if I don't notify this teen's parents?
- How much worse could this situation get if I don't reach out for help?
- How certain am I that what I'm doing is completely safe, physically, spiritually, and emotionally, for this young person?

It might help you to know that even professionals ask ourselves these same questions. I refer my clients to other therapists often. I consult with other counselors and ministry friends often. You should too.

Go "One Up"

My good friend Ela Milewska, who at the time of this writing is executive director for youth faith formation in the Archdiocese of New York, always tells her ministers, "There's nothing to lose and everything to gain by going one up." She and I are encouraging you, when a situation is even remotely questionable, to check/consult with your immediate supervisor whether that person is an administrator, pastor, associate pastor, director of religious education (DRE), or principal. For parents, you can consult another parent, your child's school counselor, or perhaps the parish youth minister if your teen is involved there. These individuals may know a trusted professional therapist who can guide you. There is absolutely *nothing* to lose and *everything* to gain by reaching out. No one, especially the young person, needs to know you're having that conversation, and you can preserve the anonymity of that individual if you're worried about confidentiality.

Limits on Confidentiality

With any conversation outside the Sacrament of Reconciliation, there are limits on how "confidential" a conversation can and should be. In most settings, educators, ministers, and other professionals do good jobs of letting young people know what those limits are. As a friend reminded me recently, "Don't let them tie your hands!" He was saying not to promise confidentiality that you cannot and should not maintain, regardless of whether they or you initiate the request. At a bare minimum, there are always at least three times when even I must, by law, break confidentiality: when teens

1. pose a threat to themselves;
2. pose a threat to another person; or
3. have experienced physical, sexual, or emotional abuse of any kind.

In addition, depending on your setting, you may be a "mandated reporter," meaning that by law and by virtue of the role you have taken on, you are required by law to report any information you have regarding a young person to your local authorities if it falls into the above three categories. In most states, there is an office of Child Protective Services. Check with your pastor, youth minister, or local law enforcement if you are not sure to whom you should report.

Other Issues that You Should Refer—No Brainers

1. *Suicidal thoughts or plan.* If teens tell you they are thinking of taking their life, this is a serious issue that needs specialized professional attention and, at a minimum, assessment by a medical or psychological professional. If you are a minister, you need to call the teen's parents and inform them. Parents, as hard as it is to hear this news about your child, it is important to get them the professional help they need. At minimum, an assessment by a medical or mental health professional can tell you if your child is really a danger to himself or herself or not and, if so, how imminent that danger is. The professional will also advise you on how to best protect your child, including admitting your child to a hospital or safeguards you can put in place at home, such as locking up guns and prescription medication.

2. *Self-harm or intent to self-harm.* If teens tell you they have hurt themselves by any type of self-injurious behavior (cutting, burning, etc.), as discussed in chapter 5, you must inform their parents so they can get their child help. For parents, again, this is something that needs attention. In most cases, self-harm is not presuicidal. It is, however, a serious cry for help and an indication that teens are responding in an unhealthy and dangerous way to situations in their life.

3. *Eating disorders.* Eating disorders are very difficult to treat. We know that the earlier these young people can have access to therapy, the better their chances are for recovery. For ministers, if you suspect a young person has an eating disorder, you might feel comfortable talking with the teen about it. Even if the young person denies any disordered eating, you should at least notify the parents of your concern and what has made you concerned. For parents, unless you are positive your child's eating is normal, you would be wise to reach out and schedule an appointment with a

counselor who can either guide you or meet with your child for an assessment.

4. *Anxiety or depression.* Because both of these, like so many things in this area of ministry and work, fall on a broad continuum from mild/not serious to severe/serious, it can be hard to tell when teens are merely sad or stressed or when they have crossed the line into anxiety and depression. Remember if it's been going on consistently for longer than two weeks, it's possible that it has crossed over the line and become a problem. Don't hesitate to consult and go one up here as well. These young people need help, and they cannot get the help they need without their parents being on board.

5. *Serious substance abuse.* It is normal for teens to experiment with substances such as alcohol and even marijuana. "Experimentation" is episodic, being once or twice. More than twice is considered abuse and is something parents have a right to know about. This is an area where you should, before the situation arises, go one up and check with your immediate supervisor as to his or her wishes or policies regarding reporting these issues. Parents, there are counselors and other mental health professionals who specialize in substance abuse. If no substance abuse counselors are in your area, any mental health professional can perform an assessment and let you know if there is a serious or budding problem.

6. *Any other serious mental health issue.* If teens tell you they are hearing voices, seeing things, hearing strange things, or doing strange things that they don't really understand, these could be symptoms of severe anxiety or depression or of a much more serious mental health issue. Again, don't hesitate to go one up for help and direction.

I'M IN OVER MY HEAD; NOW WHAT?

Now that you realize you're in over your head, that you're dealing with an issue that needs additional help, what can you do? In order to be as helpful as possible, I'll break this down into role-specific categories, because what you do in certain situations will depend on what role you play in the life of a young person.

Parents

When someone approaches parents with a concern about their child, including the children themselves, it can be tough because nothing can trigger our emotions as much as when our protective mechanism for our children gets pinged. As parents we are hardwired to protect our kids. The very thought of something bad happening to them on our watch can make us sick, literally. As such, our ingrained defense mechanisms such as denial, defensiveness, and blaming arise. I witness these in myself often and count on my wife to talk me off of my emotional ledge so I'm not too harsh on myself or on others. A few guidelines follow.

Be Aware of Your Reaction

Sometimes just being aware of *your* emotional state when you're hearing something concerning your child helps to regulate your emotions. In these situations what your child needs most is *not* an emotionally reactive parent. Your child needs you to make good, rational, and logical decisions, which can only happen when you are calm and clear headed. You won't do it perfectly and may need to talk with a friend to help you process it before taking any other action. You will probably need to take a minute to do some deep breathing.

Thank the Messenger

In the vast majority of cases when a caring adult or another young person brings you information about your child that disturbs you, they themselves have gone through emotional turmoil wondering how you're going to react or if they will lose the trust of your child. They question themselves as to whether they're overreacting; they worry they should have come to you sooner and about how you'll handle the situation with your child. They're concerned that telling may only make the problem worse.

Rarely do people report concerning behaviors to a parent to hurt you or your child. This is information you *want* as a parent. Thanking this person ensures that in the event such information comes up again in the future, they'll notify you again. Remember, you can only act on what you know. That person or group just gave you information, enabling you to act. Consider the courage it took for that. Think about how much worse things could have gotten had you not received the information.

Consult Your Spouse, Partner, or Another Parent Who Shares Your Values

If possible, do this before talking to your child. Each of us has a perspective. Although we may work hard to broaden our perspective, it still counts as one. When it comes to young people, more perspectives from trusted friends, family, and colleagues are often helpful in plotting your next actions.

Talk with Your Child

Depending on the situation, you may want to consult with a counselor or minister first to discuss how best to approach your child with this information. Regardless of the behavior, what will be remembered ten years from now will most often be *how* you handled the situation itself rather than what you did. (Being vulnerable helps.) If you're scared, tell that to your child. Hold off on disappointment (although they can usually tell in your tone and facial expressions) and anger until you've had time to settle down. Usually twenty-four hours, or a sleep cycle, are enough to get you out of "fight or flight" mode and enable you to act more based on reason than emotion. Assure your child that you love him or her. Make it clear that you recognize that the information you've received and the behaviors involved—regardless of how bad it is or seems—are clear signs that your child, and perhaps you and the whole family, need some help. Assure your child that you are committed to getting that help.

Make an Appointment with a Counselor, Pediatrician, or Other Medical/Psychological Professional

In urgent situations such as severe anxiety, depression, self-harm, suicide, or intent to harm someone else, making the call to the counselor and talking to your child need to happen quickly, so *do whichever you can first.* Sometimes it can be difficult to get in to a counselor, and most therapists or pediatricians will allow you to cancel the appointment at no cost two days or even a single day prior to the appointment.

Follow Up

Make sure to follow up with the people who notified you so they know your child is safe and getting help. They contacted you because they were worried about your child. Most often they are involved in your child's life in some capacity, and it will help them to know that the situation is being handled appropriately.

Educators, Ministers, and Other Caring Adults

If you are not the teen's parent but you are concerned about a teen, here is a process to help you validate your concern, approach the parent, and empower the parent to best help their teen.

Go to the Source

If you notice something or hear something that concerns you about a young person, try to speak with the youth directly. You might start with, "Hey, I've noticed lately that you don't seem to be yourself. How's it going?" The kid might blow it off and say, "I'm good," if the child suspects you really don't have the time or inclination to get into it. You may choose to press back gently: "Okay, well, I'm not completely convinced; I mean I've just noticed _____ [name specific behaviors in a noncondemning way to avoid raising resistance], and I care about you and just want to help if I can." If at this point the young person says, "No really, I'm good," but your gut tells you otherwise, you might say, "Okay, I'll just check back with you." Or perhaps, "Okay, well, I'm still not convinced. I'm worried/ concerned about you, and I'm here if you want to talk about anything." You might also let the young person know who else is available for support if it's needed.

Go One Up

In schools, this could be the school counselor, psychologist, or nurse if the previous two are unavailable. The school counselor has additional tools when speaking with the young person. If it's something that's not very serious and you know of another adult in a young person's life that has a better relationship with the child, you might let that person know what you're seeing and enlist his or her help. The teen may be more inclined to listen to that other individual.

Notify the Parents

Ultimately, if it's something you're concerned about and if it's one of the no brainers mentioned earlier, you need to notify the teen's parents. In some settings it may be preferable for you or your immediate supervisor to notify the parents. Here's another situation where going one up will help you to handle the situation in the most effective and helpful way for both you and the young person.

Follow Up

I'll say more about this below, but following up with the young person, whether you've notified the child's parents or not, is clearly communicating to the child that you really care. Young people know that adults are busy. They really do. So when you go out of your way and take time to check on them, they appreciate it. I know because they tell me every day! As one thirteen-year-old boy told me, "Mr. JT really cares. I know cause every now and then he pulls me aside and asks how I'm doin'. He's busy, and he still makes time for me. That's cool."

HOW TO FIND A COUNSELOR
FOR YOUR SON OR DAUGHTER

With all the titles and various licensing boards, and the multitude of options available for mental health services, it can be daunting to even begin looking for a counselor, much less finding one that will be a good fit for your teen. Below is a rough outline of a process I might use if I were looking to find a counselor for my child.

Finances

For many, paying out of pocket for counseling services is not an option. If you have insurance coverage, look into your plan to see if you have mental health coverage. If you do, make sure you understand what's covered and what's not. Review the list of people who are in network. This would include psychotherapists such as counselors (LPC [licensed professional counselor] and LMFT [licensed marriage and family therapist]), social workers (LCSW [licensed counselor social worker]), addiction counselors (LAC [licensed addiction counselor]), and psychologists (PhD and PsyD). Some may have multiple designations. For instance, LPC and LMFT is a common combination. There should be names listed under counseling, psychotherapy, and psychologists. In-network providers usually accept insurance as payment and file with your insurance provider on your behalf. You should also check to see if your insurance reimburses you, and if so at what rate, should you choose to see someone out of your network.

Check with Your Employer to See if You Have an Employee Assistance Program

Some employers contract with therapists for a set amount of sessions and provide those sessions to their employees as part of their benefit package. The upside? It's free. The downside? These employee assistance programs (known as EAPs) usually cover a limited amount of sessions that may not be enough to cover the course of treatment.

You can usually continue with that counselor if you're willing to pay the fee for service.

Check with Your Faith Community

You might also check with your church, diocese, or other religious organization as they may offer some mental health services or have a list of people they've had good experiences with. School counselors often have a list of therapists they refer to.

Network

Take the list of names from your plan and share them with friends or a counselor you may know. Ask them if they can recommend anyone from the list they think would be a good fit for your teen. Many hesitate to ask their friends because they don't want anyone to know they need a counselor or want to respect their teen's privacy. This is understandable, so you might see if you can discretely ask a trusted friend to ask for you. You might even say, "A friend of mine asked me if I knew of any counselors who worked well with teens."

Check Online Profiles

Google the names you've found. Some will have their areas of specialization on their websites. While most counselors see a variety of clientele, you can usually get a good feel for therapists by looking at their website and any publications they have produced or been featured in.

Make the Phone Call

It never hurts to call. Call the names that have surfaced from your research, and ask to speak briefly with the counselors. If you can get them on the phone, ask them if they have experience working with teens and if they enjoy working with teens. Most counselors will be honest with you. If they do not, ask if they may be able to refer you to someone who does. Then call that person. If you cannot get through to the therapist, the receptionist or office manager should be able to answer those questions for you.

Make the Initial Appointment

Most counselors will ask to meet privately with a teen's parents first. During this appointment you will get a good feel for the personality of the therapist and whether or not your teen will be a good fit with that particular therapist. While it is important for the therapist to be a good fit for parents and the teen, just because you (the parent) like the therapist does not mean your teen will connect with the therapist.

During this initial session, ask the following:

- When and how often should we expect communication from you?
- How do you handle the confidentiality?
- What exceptions do you make with teens and confidentiality?
- How can we best support you and our teen in this process?
- When will you be able to give us feedback on the frequency and duration of counseling?
- What will progress look like for you, and how quickly should we expect to see signs of progress?
- If something comes up between sessions that we feel is important for you to know, do you want us to tell you, and if so, how?

How Do I Get My Teen to Agree to Counseling?

This can be tricky. Most teens I work with don't want to come into counseling. Who can blame them. They're thinking, *Hmm . . . let me see . . . I am going to tell a perfect stranger about my most intimate thoughts, concerns, and embarrassing problems.* Some also think, *Great, now in addition to all the other things my parents think about me, they think I'm crazy and need professional help. I'm that bad off. Wow!* These are normal and to be expected. An experienced therapist knows your teen is thinking these things and has an array of tools to welcome and work with the resistance.

Encourage your teen to "just give it a shot." You can even go so far as promising them, "Look, if you don't get anything out of it after a few sessions, we can talk about stopping. Sound fair?" You can also say, "You don't have to tell the therapist anything you don't want. Now, the more open you are, the more you'll get out of it, but the therapist isn't going to make you talk." This is usually enough to convince teens to give it a try.

Understand That It Is a Process

Counseling is a process. The best results happen over time. In certain situations, there is more urgency, but for most, counseling is not working through urgent, life-threatening, or severe life-altering situations. The real work in counseling is dealing with the not-so-obvious issues lurking beneath the surface, causing the problems that you and your teen are recognizing.

Sometimes after a session or two, you realize counseling is not a good fit. That's not uncommon and quite okay. Try a different therapist. Ask that therapist for a referral to another therapist. There are a lot of factors that make for a good fit in the therapeutic relationship with teens. Don't be afraid to speak honestly with your teen's counselor if and when you or your teen thinks the relationship is not a good fit.

FOR TEACHERS, PASTORS, AND OTHER YOUTH LEADERS

For those who aren't parents, you need the help of a parent or parents to make sure the young people get the help they need. Unfortunately, I know that often when the ball is being handed off to parents it gets fumbled. It's not done in a way that gives the best chance of these kids making it into a therapist's office. Even once they're in the office, it can be dicey, but there's no chance of the young person getting the help they need if the parent doesn't follow through.

Fortunately, there are a few things you can do to increase the odds of a successful handoff.

Develop and Maintain a Curated List of Counselors Who Effectively Work with Young People

See the earlier information on "How to Find a Counselor for Your Son or Daughter." Additionally you can check with your diocese, parish, or other faith-based organization to see if there are lists of counselors who work well with young people. If a faith-based counselor is important, which it is for some, you might have a list of Catholic, Christian, and unknown/undeclared lists of counselors so you can present options to parents when giving them that information. If you make referrals often, you might consider refining your list by the following:

- Finances
  - Acceptance or not of insurance or Medicaid
  - Availability of reduced fees or a "sliding scale" based on one's ability to pay fees per session
- Structure
  - Does the therapist meet with the parents first (I usually do) and then the young person during the next session?
  - Does the therapist prefer to meet with the parents and the young person together at first?
  - How does the counselor structure the sessions?
  - If a need arises in between sessions or after hours, what is the counselor's preferred way to handle that? Are they available for phone calls and texts between sessions? (Every counselor is different in this area. Many counselors who work with teens are generous with their nonsession availability, while maintaining boundaries to enjoy their own personal life. Ask if there is a fee for nonsession calls, texts, and after-hour visits.
- Area of Specialization
  - Does the therapist have areas of specialization or preference? Often, you'll hear counselors say, "I work with kids, but I

prefer to work with adults." Make a note of that, and let the parent know this preference if you choose to refer to that person.

o Does the therapist work with younger kids? For instance, I specialize in older adolescents (fourteen to twenty-five). I don't work with youth under fourteen years.

o What approaches does the therapist use? Play therapy, art therapy, equine therapy (with horses), wolves therapy (yes, that exists, and from what I've learned, it's amazing and effective), or music therapy? These alternative approaches to traditional talk therapy work with people of all ages. In my experience, the personality and age of the teens will affect how open they will be to engaging in nontraditional techniques. That doesn't mean you shouldn't try them and encourage teens to engage. With teens who may not be very verbal, these approaches that use other modalities than the spoken word can be not only helpful and prove to be more effective but also necessary.

o Does the therapist specialize in certain areas, such as OCD, anxiety, depression, and trauma? Does the therapist have any special training in advanced therapy techniques in treating these issues?

• Experience

o How long has this individual been counseling and working with young people. In particularly complex cases, you may want to consider referring to a more experienced therapist if it's practical.

o What academic and licensing credentials does the therapist have? From which institutions?

o In what agencies or practices has the therapist worked with young people?

There are many landmines in counseling young people; a focused, intentional, and experienced therapist and a good personality fit between client and therapist help to navigate those landmines as safely and quickly as possible.

Collect and Give Out Business Cards or Digital Contact Information

The parents are much more likely to call if they don't have to search online for the contact information. I know, it's a simple search, but it's another step to already overwhelmed parents who may very well be in shock.

Ask, "Is There Anything Else I Can Do to Help Make Sure Alyssa Gets the Help She Needs?"

When parents hear about concerns for their child, they are often in shock and at times embarrassed. They may not be comfortable asking for more help from you. By asking this question, you take the initiative in making it safe for parents to accept more help and subtly suggest that more action is needed to help the teen.

Convey Hope, Seriousness, and Need for Action

You might say to parents, "Yes, this is serious, but now we know about it. Knowing this enables us to get Alyssa the help she wants and needs."

FOLLOWING UP: HOW MUCH? HOW OFTEN?

I usually suggest that following up with parents at least once is crucial. Twice would be optimal, and three to five times is usually ideal. These recommendations are based on the time and other constraints that exist in the lives of caring adults. Of course, you're free to follow up as much as you want with the parents; just be careful not to make your following up into its own problem.

You can't follow up with the young people too much. How you do it, balancing more formal follow-ups, checking on them through other people, and watching them if your setting allows for that, such as in schools or some other youth settings, should be considered. A follow-up can be as simple as saying, "Hey, just checking on you to see how you're doing." Most often the young person will say, "I'm fine," and feel cared for because you followed up. Making time for a formal one-on-one follow-up (in an appropriate setting) is valuable as it gives the young people a chance to really let you know how things are going, if they're getting better, worse, or staying the same.

Ultimately, we are not alone in working with young people, nor should we be. Our faith tradition has always emphasized and been based in caring community. In today's increasingly virtual world, we're finding it harder to be present in our physical, geographic, and even faith communities, but this doesn't mean we're better for it. It always has, still does, and always will take a village to raise young people into happy, holy, and healthy adults. Today, it takes more work to re-create the village that earlier generations were blessed with almost by default of culture. We must, for the deepest good of the young people in our care, strive to create our own villages that are appropriate to our time and locale. As people of religious faith, we ought to lean on and use the community that Catholic Christianity and today's wider culture offers us.

KEY POINTS

- When our work with young people is in the open, in the light, both they and we are above board morally, legally, and emotionally.
- Ministers need to be equipped with skills to help them pastorally care for young people, ranging from listening to making a referral to a mental health professional.

- Parents, educators, and ministers need additional tools from the social sciences that will help augment the work they do in a particular setting.
- It is important, not only for the young people in your care but also for your own self-care, that you are able to recognize when a young person needs more help than you can offer.
- When a situation is even remotely questionable, it is best to "go one up" by consulting with your immediate supervisor, whether that's an administrator, department head, clergy member, or other professional.
- Confidentiality must be violated if young people pose a threat to themselves or another person or have experienced physical, sexual, or emotional abuse. Self-harm, mention of suicide or attempts, and eating disorders are just a few scenarios that demand breaking confidentiality.
- Serious substance abuse or any other serious mental issue is also grounds for seeking the help of a medical (including, of course, mental health) professional.
- What you do in certain situations will depend on the role you play in the life of a young person.
- For parents, being aware of your reaction, thanking the messenger for bringing helpful information, consulting your spouse, and talking to your child are all best practices when you find yourself in a situation beyond your capability to handle on your own.
- There are many resources available to help you determine when your child is in need of the help of a mental health professional. Start with searching online, talking with other parents you trust, or discussing things with a school or parish counselor.
- It is often difficult to get young people to agree to counseling, but the benefits for their psychological, physical, and spiritual well-being are worth any amount of struggle and investment of time.
- Finances should never be a reason not to seek help for a young person struggling with serious mental health issues, and there are numerous resources to make quality mental health care a reality for a young person in need. Keep asking questions until you find help.

ASK YOURSELF

1. Has therapy or counseling made an impact in my own life or the life of someone I know? In what ways?
2. What are some ways that the help of a mental health professional might have positively impacted my own time as a young person?
3. Recall a situation with a young person where you felt unqualified to handle the problem presenting itself. Consider: What steps did I take to get needed help for the child?

FOR INSPIRATION AND PRAYER

What then shall we say to this? If God is for us, who can be against us? He who did not spare his own Son but handed him over for us all, how will he not also give us everything else along with him? Who shall bring a charge against God's chosen ones? It is God who acquits us. Who will condemn? It is Christ [Jesus] who died, rather, was raised, who also is at the right hand of God, who indeed intercedes for us. What will separate us from the love of Christ? Will anguish, or distress, or persecution, or famine, or nakedness, or peril, or the sword? . . . No, in all these things we conquer overwhelmingly through him who loved us. For I am convinced that neither death, nor life, nor angels, nor principalities, nor things present, nor future things, nor powers, nor height, nor depth, nor any other creature will be able to separate us from the love of God in Christ Jesus our Lord.

                                        —Romans 8:31–35, 37–39

In the world you will have trouble, but take courage, I have conquered the world.

                                        —John 16:33b

Do nothing out of selfishness or out of vainglory; rather, humbly regard others as more important than yourselves, each looking out not for his own interests, but [also] everyone for those of others.

—Philippians 2:3–4

Love is patient, love is kind. It is not jealous, [love] is not pompous, it is not inflated, it is not rude, it does not seek its own interests, it is not quick-tempered, it does not brood over injury, it does not rejoice over wrongdoing but rejoices with the truth. It bears all things, believes all things, hopes all things, endures all things.

—1 Corinthians 13:4–7

10. HEEDING THE CALL
OF THE GOOD SAMARITAN

In the Gospel of Luke, we read the parable of the good Samaritan.

> "A man fell victim to robbers as he went down from Jeru-
> salem to Jericho. They stripped and beat him and went
> off leaving him half-dead. A priest happened to be going
> down that road, but when he saw him, he passed by on
> the opposite side. Likewise a Levite came to the place,
> and when he saw him, he passed by on the opposite side.
> But a Samaritan traveler who came upon him was moved
> with compassion at the sight. He approached the vic-
> tim, poured oil and wine over his wounds and bandaged
> them. Then he lifted him up on his own animal, took him
> to an inn and cared for him. The next day he took out
> two silver coins and gave them to the innkeeper with the
> instruction, 'Take care of him. If you spend more than
> what I have given you, I shall repay you on my way back.'
> Which of these three, in your opinion, was neighbor to
> the robbers' victim?" [The expert in the Law] answered,
> "The one who treated him with mercy." Jesus said to him,
> "Go and do likewise." (Lk 10:30–37)

We find within this parable a beautiful model for accompanying
young people through difficult times. We may or may not know the
young people who cross our path, and to be honest, we may or may
not like them. Most parents have found themselves thinking or even
saying aloud at some point, "I love you, but I just don't like you right
now." Yet if we are willing, we can be open to see and respond in the
way that the good Samaritan did to the increasingly complex needs
of today's young people.

HE SEES

First, the Samaritan stops to *see* the man who has been beaten, robbed, stripped, and left on the roadside. Others do not but rather turn away from the man's need. In part 1 of this book, we explored the importance of being educated: understanding young people today, the pressures they are facing, and how they are coping in both healthy and unhealthy ways with such pressures and stressors.

This is no small point. What we see reflects what is important to us. Science has proven what Jesus says in the gospels: "Seek and you will find" (Mt 7:7, Lk 11:9). We now have scientific proof that you will ultimately find what you look for. At the base of our brain is a mechanism called the reticular activating system. This part of our brain "highlights" or brings into our conscious awareness that which is important to us. For example, the last time you were shopping for a vehicle or other item of importance to you, you probably, if you think back, can remember how much more often you began seeing that model or type of thing show up in your everyday life. You may have thought to yourself, *It sure seems that more people are driving pickups now*. When in reality, there very likely were no more trucks on the road than there were before you decided you wanted one. The simple fact that you now wanted one told your brain to highlight different makes and models. As you began to refine your choice and limit your options, your brain followed suit.

This happens in all areas of our lives. When you see young people who are hurting and struggling, it is because on some level, that is important to you and your brain has helped you notice their distress more regularly. That is a *grace*, a real gift from God. As St. John Vianney, the patron saint of parish priests, once prayed, "Lord thank you for bringing the poor to us so that we don't have to go out and look for them."

Of course, the poor are not always the material poor. In many instances young people are nowhere close to materially poor. But there is an epidemic of emotional and spiritual poverty among youth and their families today. If you don't see this, and have a heart for young people, pray for the grace to see. But be ready for what you pray for because, as Jesus said, "Seek and you will find."

It might prove helpful to revisit chapters 4–6 on occasion to sharpen your focus. Every so often, about twice a year, I review these types of warning signs, risk factors, and other symptoms so I can be sharp and recognize them when they present themselves. As Mark Twain famously said, "Don't let school interfere with your education." His wisdom is that our education, and some would suggest our most important education, continues our entire lives, long after our formal schooling has ended. I still contend that as valuable as my official training was in graduate school, some of the most valuable skills I possess I learned teaching and ministering to young people.

Just reading this book has increased your ability to see. You'll begin noticing more than you could have previously imagined now that you're tuned in.

HE CARES

You may again think, *Roy, seriously, of course he cares!* So it may surprise you to know there are many who for various reasons may see hurting youth but are not, unlike the good Samaritan, moved to compassion. If you are, again, give thanks to God for that grace. Mother Teresa prayed fervently and often: "Lord, allow my heart to break with the things that break your heart."

My hunch is that if you're reading this book, you're one who already cares. It can be tricky to care about young people. We can care for them so much that we neglect our own self-care. And while the parable doesn't give us specific detail on how the good Samaritan took care of himself, we can learn from Jesus who is described often as having "compassion" for the crowds of people who flocked to him. Jesus routinely sought silence and solitude amid what was a more-than-full ministry schedule. He understood, as should we, that while caring is a gift, we have a responsibility to ourselves, our families, our friends, our colleagues, and the young people we serve to take care of our own minds, hearts, bodies, and souls. To neglect any one of these for too long will inevitably result in burnout. Working with young people is tough. Young people don't need a flash-in-the-pan go-getter with two years of experience who leaves ministry prematurely because of self-neglect. You're not serving the young people, nor are you serving the Church in any meaningful way, by neglecting your own needs and ending up burned out.

To help prevent burnout, I recommend two resources that have been helpful to many ministers and helpers: *Riding the Dragon* by Dr. Robert Wicks and *This Wasn't in the Brochure* by Mike Patin.

The end result of burnout is a hurting person who is trying to help hurting people. What ends up happening is that hurt people (who aren't getting the help they need) don't help but instead hurt other people. Our youth need and deserve better. And so do you. When you're burnt, you stop caring or perhaps grow resentful of the very people you are expected to help.

HE RESPONDS

The Samaritan took action. He did something. He could have said to himself, "I'm not a doctor; what can I do?" Instead, he did what he could with what he had. He, with simple tools of oil, wine, and bandages, was able to comfort the afflicted man before he could get him to a place where he would receive more long-term care.

It's easy to do nothing. It takes great courage to see, care, and willingly respond with whatever gifts and tools we have at our disposal. It takes great humility to offer what we can, at times knowing it isn't enough to meet the full need or needs of that young person. It takes great strength and inner resolve to experience true compassion—merciful compassion, which is slightly different from empathy. As we observed in chapter 2, empathy means you have the ability to feel or have a similar feeling to what another person is feeling. It's wonderful to have a large well of empathy to draw from, when we can respond because we know how that situation felt for us or we can imagine how we might have felt having a similar experience.

Compassion, however, can happen with or without empathy. In being moved with compassion, one can say, "I have no idea what that's like, and I can't even begin to imagine what that would be like for me, but I want to help."

The word "compassion" literally means to "suffer with." This is important for those of us who serve youth. There will be many instances in our work with youth when we are called to suffer with, sit with, patiently wait with, walk with, and talk with in ways that don't make an obvious difference and may not seem to help at all. This is true compassion. I'm truly suffering with the other person because everything in me right now wants to fix this situation, make it better, different, but I can't. I can only accompany, walk with the person to Jesus, who alone can provide the needed healing.

LEARN TO REFER

When we care about teens, our own or someone else's and have either parented them or worked with them, it can be hard to allow someone else to also accompany them. By referring, you are not washing your hands of the teen but welcoming someone else with additional skills, training, or insight to join the village. Notice, how the good Samaritan does three things to expand the village that are also essential to making an effective referral.

First, the Samaritan moved into what could have been a messy situation. Often we do nothing because we're afraid of how messy, complicated, or complex a situation we're looking at can get. To be sure it is messy, as it could have been for the Samaritan. The Jew could have spit in his face, but he didn't. There'll be times when young people and their families don't accept our help; there may even be times when parents blame us for what's going on in their children's lives. But more often than not, we'll have opportunities to drastically influence their lives and lead them to Jesus who remains with them long after our journey with them ends.

Second, the Samaritan knew his limits. He knew what he could do and what he couldn't and didn't try to do what he wasn't capable of doing.

Third, the Samaritan did what he could with what he had. What can you do with what you've learned and the skills, insights, and natural gifts you possess? You've learned now a set of listening, dialogue, and referral skills that put you in a very small group that serves young people. The skills of listening, asking good questions, using the tools of our Catholic faith, and knowing when and how to refer young people will help more individuals than you can know. I know that sounds like a cliché, but it's important that we are reminded of the fact that most often young people whose lives we influence, and even save, will never thank us—not because they're not grateful but because their lives move them on from us so quickly. For every one young person who thanks you, writes you, or otherwise expresses gratitude, you can add to that another twenty-five who feel the same way but just haven't told you. As you model healthy, vulnerable, and affirming communication, young people will learn from you and be more likely to express care and gratitude to you and others in their lives. When this happens, the gap between adults and teens that causes fear on both sides begins to close.

HE CONTINUES ON HIS JOURNEY

The Samaritan doesn't adopt the Jewish man or bring him into his own home. By knowing his limits he was able to recognize the Jewish man needed more help than he could offer at that moment, and he found for him a place where he could get the next level of care. We don't know if the innkeeper ended up doing the same upon closer examination because we never get to hear the end of the story. But Jesus' command to us is to do like the good Samaritan. We too, like him, are on our own journey with the Lord and with our families and friends and others in our faith community. Our lives should never be centered on the work we do with young people. It's not healthy for them, nor is it healthy for us. When our lives are centered around work, young people see this and develop a warped sense of what it means to be Christian; live in community; be a healthy, whole adult; and minister either voluntarily or professionally in the Church. If they see you "living" at school or church, they will wonder (I know because they tell me) if you have a life, and when they conclude you don't or that you're neglecting your life and the people closest to you, they don't feel special and cared for; they feel used, as if they're your next best option because you can't or don't have a life elsewhere. This is even true for ordained and professed priests and religious who have promised celibacy or taken vows of chastity. When young people see that you have boundaries and that you have a personal life, they respect you more because they sense you're healthier. And they are right to do so.

HE FOLLOWS UP

When we successfully or unsuccessfully refer or get young people and their parents to the help they need, our role doesn't end. If we truly care about that young person, we would make an effort, like the Samaritan, to return to them and check in. This may be difficult, especially if we've had to stretch or break their trust by notifying their parents of something we've observed. They may not even want to talk with us, or they may have pulled away slightly because their energy is needed elsewhere while getting the additional help they need. Regardless of how young people or their families respond, they will still feel on some level grateful for our compassion and making an effort to follow up. Even if we mess up the handoff, our sincerity in caring compassion can absolve a multitude of sins.

~~~~~~~~~~~~~~

The Church needs your vision, your heart, your gifts, your skills, and your presence in the lives of young people today more than ever before. This generation of young people needs eyes that can see the signs and the needs, hearts that care and are willing to respond, and minds that have healthy boundaries and limits. By reading this book, you've made a generous investment of your time. Thank you. By practicing the tools and techniques you've learned, you will make a contribution beyond your wildest imagination to the young people you accompany. Please step in. I look forward to joining you as we together walk with teens along the journey of faith.

NOTES

PREFACE

1. "Child Poverty," National Center for Children in Poverty, Columbia University Mailman School of Public Health, accessed August 25, 2018, http://www.nccp.org.

1. HOW BIG IS THE PROBLEM?

1. "Prevalence of Major Depressive Episode among Adolescents," National Institute of Mental Health, last updated November 2017, https://www.nimh.nih.gov.

2. Jayne O'Donnell and Anne Saker, "Teen Suicide Is Soaring: Do Spotty Mental Health and Addiction Treatment Share Blame?" *USA Today*, March 19, 2018, https://www.usatoday.com.

3. "Suicide Statistics," American Foundation for Suicide Prevention, accessed September 8, 2018, https://afsp.org (taken from "Centers for Disease Control and Prevention [CDC] Data and Statistics Fatal Injury Report for 2016").

4. Alicia Vanorman and Beth Jarosz, "Suicide Replaces Homicide as Second-Leading Cause of Death among US Teenagers," Population Reference Bureau, June 9, 2016, https://www.prb.org.

5. John Peterson, Stacey Freedenthal, Christopher Sheldon, and Randy Andersen, "Nonsuicidal Self Injury in Adolescents," *Psychiatry* 5, no. 11 (November 2008): 20–26, https://www.ncbi.nlm.nih.gov.

6. "What Is Bullying: Frequency of Bullying," Stopbullying.gov, last updated July 26, 2018, https://www.stopbullying.gov.

7. "Statistics: Bullying Statistics," National Voices for Equality, Education, and Enlightenment, accessed September 8, 2018, https://www.nveee.org.

8. "Adoption Statistics," Adoption Network Law Center, accessed September 8, 2018, https://adoptionnetwork.com.

9. "Adoption Statistics."

10. Teresa Wiltz, "Why More Grandparents Are Raising Children," Stateline, Pew Charitable Trusts, November 2, 2016, http://www.pewtrusts.org.

11. "LGBTQ Family Fact Sheet," Family Equality Council, US Census Bureau, November 6, 2017, https://www2.census.gov/cac/nac/meetings/2017-11/LGBTQ-families-factsheet.pdf.

5. RECOGNIZING ANXIETY AND DEPRESSION

1. "Depression," National Institute of Mental Health, last updated February 2018, https://www.nimh.nih.gov.

2. "Adolescent Mental Health Basics," US Department of Health and Human Services, last updated March 14, 2018, https://www.hhs.gov.

3. National Institute of Mental Health, "Depression."

ROY PETITFILS is a Catholic author, speaker, and psychotherapist in private practice.

His books include *What Teens Want You to Know (But Won't Tell You)*, *What I Wish Someone Had Told Me About the First Five Years of Marriage*, *God Wears Running Shoes*, and *A Practical Guide to High School Campus Ministry*.

Petitfils has more than twenty-five years of experience ministering to youth and young adults in parishes, dioceses, and schools. He has spoken to youth and adults in more than seventy-five dioceses in the United States and Canada, and has given keynote addresses at numerous national and regional conferences, including USCCB Convocation of Catholic Leaders, NCCYM, and NCYC. Petitfils also spoke at TEDx in 2016 and is host of the popular *Today's Teenager Podcast*.

He has a bachelor's degree in liberal arts from St. Joseph Seminary College. He did graduate work in spirituality and theology at Pontifical University of St. Thomas Aquinas and earned a master's degree in community and school counseling from the University of Louisiana Lafayette.

Petitfils lives in Lafayette, Louisiana, with his wife, Mindi, and their children.

www.roypetitfils.com
Facebook: roypetitfils
Twitter: @roypetitfils
Instagram: roypetitfils
Pinterest: @roypetitfils

AVE

AVE MARIA PRESS

Founded in 1865, Ave Maria Press,
a ministry of the Congregation of
Holy Cross, is a Catholic publishing
company that serves the spiritual and
formative needs of the Church and its
schools, institutions, and ministers;
Christian individuals and families; and
others seeking spiritual nourishment.

For a complete listing of titles from

Ave Maria Press

Sorin Books

Forest of Peace

Christian Classics

visit www.avemariapress.com

AVE MARIA PRESS
Notre Dame, IN
A Ministry of the United States Province of Holy Cross